# Estevanico

## The First Black Man in America

Stephen J. Vicchio, Ph.D.

Wisdom
Editions
Minneapolis

**Wisdom Editions**

Minneapolis
FIRST EDITION May 2023

Cover image: *Estevanico* by Sam Patrick. Courtesy of Miriam Matthews photograph collection (Collection 1889). Library Special Collections, Charles E. Young Research Library, UCLA.

Printed in the United States of America

10 9 8 7 6 5 4 3 2 1

ISBN: 978-1-960250-82-7

Cover and interior design: Gary Lindberg

# Contents

Temporally, New Mexico has often been divided by archeologists into the troublesome binary of "prehistoric" and "historic;" or framed by historians into distinct periods: Pre-Contact, Spanish Colonial, Mexican Territorial, and American. All fail to capture the complexity of cycles and the transitions that lead up to and follow events, both cataclysmic and ordinary.

—George Lena Pena, *Decolonizing New Mexico*

Also by Stephen J. Vicchio

*Muslim Slaves in the Chesapeake: 1634 to 1865*
*Mala'ika: Angels in Islam*
*Evil and Suffering in the Bible*
*The Akedah or Sacrifice of Isaac*
*Evil in World Religions*
*Alexander Hamilton's Religion*
*The Idea of the Demonic*

# Estevanico

## The First Black Man in America

# Preface

In this Preface, we will assemble a few other comments regarding my claim that Estevanico was the first Black man in America. In the Introductory Essay to follow, we will show that several other Black men were given the same moniker in the late fifteenth and early sixteenth centuries. We also indicate that eight other Africans have been suggested in terms of winning the award of "First." In the Introductory Essay, we mention:

1. Reports of Black babies being born in St. Augustine, Florida
2. Pedro Alonso Niño
3. An early Black slave of Hernando de Soto's who is said to have lived in Alabama
4. Juan Garrido
5. John Punch
6. William Tucker
7. Slaves of Balboa
8. "Antonio," or Anthony Johnson

We will speak of extant evidence of these eight Black men to come to some general conclusions about them. Regarding de Soto's slave, a man named "Robles" apparently was a Christian runaway from de Soto's camp and eventually settled in Coosa, Alabama.[1] Another of his slaves, a man named Johan Biscayan, spent time in Georgia in a place called Ulibahall.[2]

In a letter dated April 20, 1537, King Charles V gave Hernando de Soto permission to take "fifty Africans, a third of them female, to Florida."[3] It is likely that Robles and Biscayan were both among this fifty, but they would have come after 1537, and that is long after Estevanico arrived in 1528.

Regarding extant materials on Juan Garrido, we know that he wrote a document to the King of Spain that consists of 240 words that he called a *Probanza*. He wrote the document from Mexico City and spoke of the many adventures he had engaged in, including San Juan, Puerto Rico, and the island of Cuba in service to the *Perpetual Rey*.[4] In the opening of his *Probanza*, Garrido indicated that it was dated September 27, 1538, but again, that is long after Estevanico arrived in the New World in 1528.

In the Introductory Essay, we make arguments against the claims of primacy in regard to Blacks in St. Augustine, John Punch and William Tucker in Virginia, as well as "Antonio," or Anthony Johnson, who arrived in Virginia, by all available evidence, from Angola in 1621.[5]

Again, there is a wealth of extant information on Pedro Alonso Niño and his alleged navigation of Columbus' ship, the *Santa Maria*, in 1492. At the Spanish Court at the time was a man named Peter Martyr who wrote many letters to his friends about the first voyage of Columbus to the New World. Copies of these letters were sent to officials in Venice and were printed in 1504.[6]

Peter Martyr's letters do mention Pedro Alonso Niño, but he was neither described as a "Negro," nor as a "Slave." Subsequent publishing of the letters also did not identify Niño that way, nor is he called a "Navigator," nor a "pilot," as they often were called in those days. Earlier, we mentioned the conclusion about Pedro Niño made by scholar Vincent Cassidy in which he wrote in a 1959 article:

> The legend of the Negro pilot is duly recorded in many books on Negro history. Some say, "he was." Some, "he might have been," and some, "even if he was not." But few, if any, go into any detail.[7]

Nevertheless, there is evidence that Pedro Niño, along with Christopher Guerra, received permission from Bishop Juan Rodríquez de Fonseca to explore the Gulf of Paria. On the island of Margarita, they bargained for many pearls before they made their way to the Cubagua Islands. They returned to Spain in 1500, but they were imprisoned because it was believed that they did not hand over all they had collected. Eventually, Niño was exonerated and was set free.[8]

We can be certain that Pedro Niño had dark skin. Some sources suggest he had a White father and a slave mother. One other item we know about Pedro Alonso Niño is that two of his brothers, Francisco, younger, and Juan, older, were also on the ship manifests of Columbus' 1492 voyage.

Some may count Pedro Niño as the first Black man in what will become the United States, but he is neither called a "Slave" nor a "Negro" in the available evidence. In fact, if Peter Martyr's original letters are considered as evidence—and they are not available—the copies that are available do not mention slavery nor Blackness in regard to Pedro Alonso Niño.

Once again, this leaves us with the Moroccan slave Estevanico, or "Little Stephen," sold by the Portuguese to the Spanish Crown in 1513 and then designated as a slave in the New World beginning in 1527–1528 and continuing as a slave until 1536 when he was set free, three years before his demise by the Zuni Indians.

There are at least another half a dozen African or "Mulatto" men mentioned on the manifests of early explorers' ships. But many of these Black individuals performed their services in places like Peru, Costa Rica, Honduras, Panama, and Chile. But only Juan Garrido and Estevanico had discoveries in what is now the United States. The former in Baja, California, and the latter in Florida, Texas, Arizona and New Mexico.

Two other issues deserve some comment. These may be called Presentism and Sympathetic Magic, or the Laws of Similarity and Contagion. "Presentism" is the belief that the moral values and beliefs of the present are superior to those of the past and that we now have gotten issues, such as race and gender, under control because now we know the truth about them. Thus, those in the past were wrong about race and gender, and with the passage of time, we now have the proper and truthful understanding of those issues.

In several articles and in a book called *Racial Oppression and Social Control*, scholar Theodore W. Allen asks a simple but meaningful question, "When did Europeans begin to see themselves as 'White,' and their slaves as 'Black?'" Another way to ask the same question is this: When did the word "White" first begin to be employed in America as a token of social status? Dr. Allen's answer to that question is enlightening.

His answer to that question is from a Virginia law passed in 1691 that referred to "English and other White women."[9] On September 8, 2000, Theodore W. Allen was interviewed on *The Tom Pope Show* that airs on WSMX FM radio. In that interview, Dr. Allen observed:

> When the first Africans arrived in Virginia in 1619, there were no "White" people there. People living in the colony at the time were English. They had been English when they left England and naturally they and their Virginia-born children were English as well. They were not "White."

In the same interview, Professor Allen goes on to say:

> White identity has to be carefully taught, and it would only be after the passage of some crucial six decades that the word would appear as a synonym for European-American.

When we speak of race in the twenty-first century, it is inconceivable that the light-skinned residents of Virginia did not see themselves as "White." Nevertheless, the first documented proof of when the word "White" began to be used that way is the year 1691. This raises the question, of course, of when Black slaves began to see themselves as "Black" and when light-skinned colonists began to refer to their captives as "Black."

For our purposes, it also raises the question of whether Estevanico understood himself as being Black or as being a man from Morocco. Whatever the answer to that question is, it should be clear, however, that Presentism has raised its ugly head in the debate about race in America, and that is true in regard to the issue of gender, as well.

The final issue to discuss regarding Estevanico, or "Little Stephen," is an issue that will become important when talking about the murder of the slave from Morocco is what we have labeled "Sympathetic Magic" in the Introductory Essay to this study. According to Sir James Frazer in the *Golden Bough*, the idea of Sympathetic Magic is a confluence of what he calls the "Law of Similarity" and the "Law of Contagion." We reintroduce these ideas because they will become important when understanding some of the interactions that Estevanico and his colleagues had with the pre-literate people of the Great Plains of America.

Remember that the great anthropologist Frazer defines the law of similarity as "like produces like." And the Law of Contagion as "Once two things have a cause-and-effect relationship, those two things will permanently remain that way." The process of making a Voodoo doll to look like an enemy and then placing pins in the doll to harm the enemy is an illustrative example of sympathetic magic.

Another fine example of the phenomenon is the very early man-made prehistoric images created in the cave complexes of Altamira, Spain, and Lascaux, France, between 20,000 and 15,000 BCE. The painting of animals discovered there displays an acuity of visual perception and drawing skill that seem to imply a "Sympathy" for the animals.[10]

Another great cultural anthropologist, Henri Breuil (1877–1961), used the word "Magic" in describing the cave drawings, denoting an "archetypal belief held by many so-called 'Primitive' societies that to possess the image of the animal—so vital to the hunter's own survival—ensures a degree of human control over the animal's fate."[11] Professor Breuil wrote several books on the cave of Altamira and the history of cave art in general. Most of these were written from the 1930s to 1950s.

We introduced the subject of sympathetic magic into our discussion of Estevanico because many of the Native Americans he encountered clearly were believers in the Law of Similarity and the Law of Contagion, as we shall see, for example, when the slave from Morocco dealt with the Zuni Indians at the end of his life in Cibola, or Hawikuh.[12]

# Introductory Essay

In 1527 an expedition sailed from Spain commanded by Pánfilo de Narváez to explore the northern shore of the Gulf of Mexico. After a short stop in Hispaniola—the current Dominican Republic and Haiti—and then Cuba, some three hundred men landed at a place on the coast of Florida that most likely was the Sarasota Bay on April 14, 1528.

Estevanico's Route 1527-1539

Most of the Narváez expedition moved inland but soon divided, one part continuing by land while the other explored the coast by sea. The two groups met hostile Native Americans. A series of hardships plagued the mission's men. They ate their horses to alleviate hunger and drank salt water. They also experienced sickness and the threat of desertion.

Eventually, only four members of the Narváez expedition remained. These were Álvar Núñez Cabeza de Vaca, Andrés Dorantes de Carranza, a Spanish nobleman named Castillo, and Estevanico, a Negro slave owned by Señor Dorantes. These four survivors spent some six years living as slaves or servants of the American Indians in what is now Western Louisiana or Eastern Texas. The group finally escaped and crossed over the Rio Grande into what was then Mexican territory in 1536.

In this study, the man we will call Estevanico (1499–1539) most likely was born "Mustafa Zemmouri." He is the first known person of African descent to have arrived in the present-day continental United States. As mentioned earlier, he was one of only four survivors of the Spanish Narváez expedition, and he traveled with explorer Cabeza de Vaca across northern New Spain (the present-day US Southwest and Northern Mexico).

This is the story, then, of the Negro man known as "Estevanico," or "Little Stephen" in Portuguese. He was a scout and ambassador more than a guide for the Narváez expedition. The Negro went ahead for the purpose of sending back reports of the importance of the pueblos and towns he found in what would become the American Southwest. Before we get to an analysis of Estevanico, the slave of Señor Dorantes, we must first make some observations about why we claim that he was the first Black man in America.

## Estevanico: The First Black Man in America

> As long as the concept of an African American is current and as long as African American history is seen as beginning with the enslavement in Africa, then Esteban [Estevanico] is important because he is the first African American.

> —Robert Goodwin, *Crossing the Continent 1527–1540*

This is the story of a man named Estevanico, a Portuguese diminutive for the name Esteven or Stephen. Thus, it means "Little Stephen." The same man also answered to many other names, including:

- Black Stephen
- Esteban
- Estebanico
- Esteben de Dorantes
- Esteven the Moor or *Esteben El Moro* in Spanish
- Little Stephen the Ship-Wrecked or *Estebanico El naufragio*
- Little Stephen, the Moor or *Estebanico El Mauro*
- Mustafa Zemmouri
- Mustapha of Zemmouri or *Mustapha El-Azemmouri*
- Stephen the Black
- Stephen the Moor or *Esteban el Mora* in Spanish
- Stephen the Moor or *Esteven El moro* in Portuguese

This list could also include several other monikers that Estevanico may have answered to. Among many scholars, the Black man is referred to as "Estevanico de Azemmour" or "Little Stephen from Azemmour." This name, from the outset, has several cultural identities that may help us identify this man from Morocco.

This combination of names calls to mind the Spanish and Portuguese practices of naming. If we add the fact that Azemmour is a city in Morocco, it adds to the Black man's identity with an undeniable "Moorish" blend to his name. The Moorish claim is further supported by the similarities of the names *Estevan* and *Esteban* in Portuguese and Spanish to the Arabic name *Mustapha*, a name in North Africa and Iberia that is seen as the equivalent of Stephen.

These combined East-West elements of Estevanico's name have resulted in the conferring of the various names listed above to the Moroccan man that is now called the "First Black Man in America."

These various elements of identity that came together in Estevanico's short life—he died at age thirty-eight or thirty-nine—also were combined with a host of other identities, as we shall see in this study of his life. Among these other identities, we may list the following that Estevanico was:

- A slave
- First freed Black slave in America
- An adventurer
- A healer
- A scout or guide
- An interpreter
- A translator
- An explorer
- An unrecognized Conquistador
- A possible descendant of the Hausa Tribe of Mali

In her first-person narrative, written to the King of Spain, as the person of his servant, Estevanico, Helen Rand Parish suggested that although our hero was born in Morocco, his family may have migrated here from Mali and, if they did, were most likely members of the Hausa Tribe. If this were true, that would explain why Estevanico's skin color appeared to be much darker than other North Africans of the sixteenth century from Tunisia, Algeria and Morocco.

Ms. Parish also identified Estevanico's family with the kingdom of Mansa Musa, who ruled Mali from 1312 until 1337. Musa's empire continued well into the time of Estevanico and his parents. In fact, the kingdom existed until the year 1670, more than a century after Estevanico's death in 1539.

It is likely that Estevanico also had *Doukkali* stock in his blood. Doukkali is the name of the tribe that populated the region of Azemmour and al-Jadida. Al-Jadida, called *Mazagan* by the North Africans, is a Portuguese fortified walled city southwest of Casablanca. In this sense, perhaps we should add a Berber/Punic element to our collection of identities for Estevanico, as well as the indigenous people of Morocco, and because of his color, maybe a sub-Saharan flavor of identity.

In much of modern scholarship about Estevanico, countless pages have been spent on whether the Moroccan slave was a "Negro" or a "Moor." In his 1940 essay entitled "Estevanico," Rayford Logan pointed out that Cabeza de Vaca often referred to his companion as a "Negro," as did Pedro de Castañeda. But Cleve Hallenbeck claimed, "He was a Moor and not a Negro."[13]

Whatever way we answer that identity question, however, the Islamic Moorish tradition, as well as the fact that his skin was black, by most accounts of his contemporaries, though one source said it was "brown," these two traditions must also be included in ascertaining the collective identity that went into the making of the Moroccan man known as Estevanico, or "Little Stephen."

However, we must remember that the late twentieth and early twenty-first centuries' penchant, primarily to relate identity to skin color, was not a custom and belief of Moroccans and people of Iberia in the early sixteenth century. Identity, for those people, went far beyond the amount of melanin in one's skin.

Estevanico is known today for several reasons besides being the first Black man to set foot in what would eventually become the United States. He is also remembered because he was a slave, long before the "twenty-odd Blacks" who came to Virginia in 1619.[14] Another reason Estevanico is important is that he was the slave scout who led an expedition over what is today Arizona, Texas, New Mexico and Northern Mexico. Estevanico was also the first non-native person to enter what would become Arizona and New Mexico.[15]

This introductory narrative in particular and the study of Estevanico will unfold in the following parts:

- Some background information on Estevanico.
- An account of the early and later life of the Moroccan slave.
- An account of Estevanico's scouting forays into Mexico and the Great West of the US.
- A description and discussion of the death of Estevanico.
- The subsequent influences of the life and times of Estevanico.

However, before we turn to those five parts, or chapters, we will first discuss our claim that the Moroccan was the first Black man in what will become the continental United States, although some scholars and other thinkers maintain that Estevanico was not the first at all.

Indeed, several other African and European-born Black men have also been given credit for being the first Black man in what would become the United States. We will mention eight of these examples, offer a critique of each and then conclude that the Moroccan slave known as Estevanico is the better choice.

These eight suggestions are the following:

1. An early Black slave of de Soto who is said to have lived in Alabama.
2. Pedro Alonzo Niño, a "Negro" who is said to have been on Christopher Columbus' first voyage to the New World in 1492.
3. Thirty slaves of Balboa who are said to have accompanied him on his discovery of the Pacific Ocean.
4. A Black man named Juan Garrido, a Spanish conquistador, born in Africa around 1480.
5. John Punch (1640) was the first to be "perpetually enslaved." (Virginia colony)
6. William Tucker, the first Black child born in the Jamestown Colony. Baptized January 3, 1625.
7. Reports of early births of Black children in the continental US (January 3, 1606) in St. Augustine, Florida.
8. Anthony Johnson, a Virginia and Maryland slave owner.

At the Convent of San Francisco in Moguer, Spain, there is a bronze monument of Pedro Niño (number 2 in the above list). He is dressed in a conquistador costume with a pilot's cap on his head. He sits at a table on which there is an hourglass on the left and a lantern on the right. There is a medieval-looking map spread out on the desk. Niño's left hand rests on the table, and there is a stylus in his right hand. His legs and feet are beneath the table. Niño's face has a strong nose, thick lips and strong eyes. There is no indication, however, that he is Black.

William Tucker (number 6 in the above list) is sometimes referred to as the "First Black Man in America" because his birth and baptism were the first ever recorded of a Black child in colonial records. He was born in November of 1624 and baptized in Virginia on January 3, 1625. But he was not the first Black man in what would become the United States.

Item number 4 on our list, Juan Garrido, like Estevanico, was born in West Africa around 1480. A document notarized from 1538 relates that Garrido moved from Africa to Lisbon, Portugal, of his own volition and traveled as a *horro*, that is "a free man."[16] He sailed from Seville, Spain, around 1508 and arrived at Hispaniola—as Estevanico did—and later lived in San Juan, Puerto Rico.[17]

Garrido also fought with and for Juan Ponce de Leon in the colonization of both Cuba and Puerto Rico while Ponce de Leon searched for the "Fountain of Youth," and he participated in Hernán Cortés's destruction of the Aztec Empire. Garrido came to the New World long after Estevanico's arrival in 1528, but he appears to have possessed very little of the traits attributed to the Moroccan slave, as we shall see later in this study.[18]

There are no extant records of Black children born in St. Augustine, Florida, which began as a land grant from the king in 1565, but that was long after the arrival of Estevanico. There is evidence that John Punch of Virginia was the first man to be declared in court on July 9, 1640, "perpetually enslaved," or a slave for life.[19] Although the court's decision of Mr. Punch's case is clearly a "First," it does not merit him the moniker of "First Black Man in the United States."

Similarly, we do not know the name of de Soto's slave who may have settled in Alabama. There are references to him in the literature, but nothing to establish he was the first. Balboa appears to have been accompanied to the Pacific by several Africans, but we do not know their names.[20]

The Virginia slave, *Antonio*, who later changed his name to "Anthony Johnson," should be awarded as the first Black man to do something in what will become the United States. But Johnson would be given the award because he was a former slave who later became a slave owner.[21]

Finally, Pedro Alonso Niño (ca. 1455–1505) was an Afro-Spanish explorer who reportedly helped navigate the *Santa Maria*, one of Cristopher Columbus' three ships in his first voyage to the New World that left the port of Palos, Spain, in August of 1492.[22] There is now a monument to Pedro Alonso Niño at the Convent of San Francisco in Moguer, Spain.[23]

Niño is also said to have accompanied Columbus on his third voyage to the New World that, among other things, saw the discovery of Trinidad and the mouth of the Orinoco River. Some sources indicate that the "Negro" was employed as a translator in and around Trinidad, for the islands' inhabitants were of West African origins, as the "Negro" was, as well.

In a 1959 essay written by Vincent Cassidy entitled "Columbus and 'The Negro'," Cassidy wrote the following about "Pedro Alonso, the Negro."

> The legend of the Negro pilot is duly recorded in many books in Negro history. Some say, "he was," some, "he might have been," and some even said, "Even if he was not." But few of them go into any detail.[24]

The skepticism of Vincent Cassidy is warranted. There is very little collaborative evidence to make a conclusion that a Black man was the chief navigator and pilot on Columbus's initial voyage to the New World that commenced in the late summer of 1492. At this point of the scholarship, the matter is still up to some debate.

There is some evidence that an Angolan man named Sebastian Rodriquez, born around 1642, came to what would become New Mexico in 1692. Records indicate that Governor Diego de Vargas—the man the Spanish put in charge of resettling New Mexico—and after the Pueblo Revolt in 1680, brought Rodriquez with him when they traveled north. Mr. Rodriquez reportedly had been the drummer and the town crier for the garrison in El Paso, Texas.

Another interesting fact about Sebastian Rodriquez is that records show that in 1697, he was able to purchase a piece of property in Santa Fe, New Mexico. One of his sons continued in the role of Santa Fe's Town Crier. Another of Rodriquez's sons became one of the first Black settlers in the north village of *Las Trampas* between Santa Fe and Taos, New Mexico. But again, Sebastian Rodriquez came to the Southwest more than thirty years after Estevanico, so he clearly was not the first Black man in the region.

This leaves us with the name of Estevanico, or "Little Stephen," who was born sometime between 1499 and 1503. There is no doubt that he had black skin by all available accounts. It is also likely that he was born in Morocco, as we shall see in the first section of this study on the life of Estevanico, to which we shall turn next.

Beyond these other possible "firsts," a recent book by Andrés Reséndez called *The Other Slavery* states that long before the year 1619 and the "twenty or so Africans" brought to the Virginia colony in August of that year, the enslavement of Native Americans had gone on since the middle of the fifteenth century and between that time and the end of the Civil War, between two and five million Native peoples had been made slaves in what became the United States. We will say more about Professor Reséndez and his book later in the study. In the meantime, however, he has shown that slavery began in America long before those championed in the *New York Times*' "1619 Project."[25]

## Background Information on Estevanico

In this second section of this Introductory Essay on Estevanico, we will describe and discuss four separate pieces of background information necessary to understand the other sections of this essay. This background material consists of the following:

1. The coming of Islam to the Iberian Peninsula.
2. The coming of Judaism to the Iberian Peninsula.
3. What has come to be known as the "Edict of Expulsion" in 1492.
4. A description and discussion of the city of Azemmour, Morocco, where Estevanico was born and raised until he was a late adolescent or early adult.

One piece of background information that is essential in understanding the life of Estevanico is the arrival of Islam into the Iberian Peninsula in the eighth century CE. In the year 711, a Muslim force consisting of Arab and Berber warriors entered the Iberian Peninsula from North Africa.[26] They were about seven thousand strong under the general leadership of Tariq Ibn Ziyad and were loyal to the Umayyad Emir of Damascus, al-Walid the First.

At the Battle of Guadalete, Tariq's army defeated that of Visigoth King Roderick.[27] In the following year, the Muslim governor of North Africa, a man named Musa Ibn Nusayr, followed Tariq's troops with an army of five thousand. A short time after their arrival, Nusayr controlled the cities of Sidonia and Seville in Spain and Mertola in Portugal.[28]

Over the next two years, Nusayr took control of Jaen, Murcia, Granada and Sagunto and much of the southern Iberian Peninsula, particularly the Lower Ebro Valley. This region was now called *Al-Andalus*. By 717, Cordoba had become the capital of the Muslim Al-Andalus. By 720, the Umayyad Arabs had control of Barcelona, Spain, and the French Roman port city of Narbonne.

By the year 785 CE, the Umayyads had built the Great Mosque of Cordoba on the grounds of a former Visigoth church. Three years later, Abd ar-Rahman the First, the founder of the Umayyad Emirate of Cordoba, died and was succeeded by Hisham the First.[29]

Around 800, Charlemagne had taken Barcelona and was granted the title "Holy Roman Emperor" by Pope Leo III in order to guarantee the protection of Rome from the Lombards in the early ninth century.[30] In 809 and 810, an Umayyad prince defeated and executed Tumius, a Muslim rebel who had taken control of Lisbon in Portugal.[31]

Over the next several centuries, the southern region of the Iberian Peninsula alternately was under the control of the Muslims and the Christians. By the time of Estevanico's birth in Azemmour, Morocco, around 1500, it was controlled by the Portuguese. This brings us to the settlement of Judaism in the Iberian Peninsula, our next topic of background information for the life of Estevanico.

Around the year of Estevanico's birth in 1500, there were twenty thousand inhabitants in the city of Azemmour. About three thousand were Jews. They mostly worked as fishermen and craftsmen, though there were also some wealthy merchants and moneylenders. Most of these wealthy Jews in Azemmour were exiles from Portugal who migrated to Morocco after 1496. The Jews of Azemmour subsequently were raided by the Spanish, but up until 1513, the city was controlled by Portugal.[32]

On June 14, 1514, the Spanish conferred a grant of privilege on the Jews of Azemmour. This also fixed the taxes to be paid to the crown of Spain. At the time, the Jewish community was led by Rabbi Joseph Adibe. Among the Jewish surnames in Azemmour at the time were: Adibe, Roti, Valensi, Buros, Rodriquez and Cordilha.[33]

These Jews came to be called "Marranos." They were welcomed in Azemmour and were allowed to settle in the interior of Morocco, where they could secretly return to their Jewish faith.

David Ha-Reuveni arrived in Portugal in 1525. His grandiose plans inspired messianic visions of the martyr, Solomon Molcho. Reuveni claimed to be a descendant of the tribe of Reuben from a Jewish state in Arabia. Reuveni gained the favor of Pope Clement VII and King John III of Portugal and had a plan to lead a Jewish army against Islam in Palestine.[34]

During the reign of King John III, Reuveni ordered the evacuation of all Jews to Arzila and compensated them for their troubles. A community of Jews was re-established in 1780. Azemmour continued to have a Jewish population until most wealthy Jews emigrated from Morocco after 1948 and the establishment of the Jewish state. By 1968, no Jews were living in Azemmour.[35] This brings us to the Edict of Expulsion of 1492, our next item of background information for the life of Estevanico.

The city of Azemmour is on the Atlantic coast of Morocco, about seventy kilometers, or forty-seven miles, southwest of Casablanca. It is situated in what is called the "Dukala coastline." The current population of Azemmour is about forty thousand, twice that of when Estevanico was born around 1500.

During the fifteenth century, the Portuguese were in the process of securing coastal sites and were able to offer protection to cities like Azemmour. Later, when the governor of the city refused to pay tribute to Lisbon, a Portuguese army was sent to Azemmour and what was called the "Battle of Azemmour" ensued. In fact, the explorer Magellan was a soldier in that battle. Eventually, however, Portugal abandoned Azemmour, mostly for economic reasons.

Estevanico of Morocco was born, enslaved and then sold to the Spanish, ending up as a scout and a linguist for the crown of Spain. A bust of Estevanico is part of a historical sculpture series in El Paso, Texas. As one walks around Azemmour, even today, one is impressed by the walls, the kasbah, or castle, and the late medieval architecture. We will say more about Estevanico's influence on art in Chapter Seven of this study.

The Edict of Expulsion promulgated by Ferdinand and Isabella of Spain went public in the week of April 29, 1492. The charter declared that no Jews were permitted to remain within the Spanish kingdom. Jews who wished to convert to Christianity were encouraged by the crown and were welcome to stay. It did not matter how rich or poor they were. All Jews had to convert or leave the Iberian Peninsula.[36]

After sketching out the many titles of Ferdinand and Isabella, the Edict goes on to describe the "great injury, detriment, and opprobrium of our Holy Catholic Faith." In the third paragraph of the Edict, the text proclaims:

> Nor withstanding that we were informed of the great part of this before now and we knew that the true remedy for all these injuries and inconveniences was to prohibit all interactions between the said Jews and Christians and to banish them from all our kingdoms, we desired to content ourselves by commanding them to leave all cities, towns, and villages of Andalusia where it appears they have done the greatest injury, believing that they would be sufficient so that those of the other cities, towns, and villages of our kingdoms and lordships, would cease to do and commit the aforesaid acts.[37]

Thus, shortly before the birth of Estevanico around 1500, King Ferdinand and Queen Isabella of Spain had banished all Jews from their kingdoms. This brings us to one final piece of background information on the life of Estevanico, some observations about the city in which he was born, that is, Azemmour, Morocco, around the turn of the sixteenth century.

Originally, the town of Azemmour was a Phoenician port. In those days, it was called *Azama*, a Berber or Punic word that means "wild olive tree."[38] Azemmur is on the left bank of the Oum Er-Rbia River. *Azama* was Latinized to become *Asama* and eventually the modern name for the city, *Azemmour*.

Before the year 1486, Azemmour was a dependent state of the King of Fez. In that year, the inhabitants of the city became the vassals and tributaries of King Jao II of Portugal. Around 1513, the governor of Azemmour was Moulay Zayam, who refused to pay tribute to the Portugal crown and he mustered a powerful and well-equipped army to fight the Portuguese.[39]

The Portuguese responded, however, by sending a large fleet of five hundred ships and fifteen thousand soldiers. This army was led by James, Duke of Braganza, and on September 1, 1486, he conquered the city of Azemmour with little or no resistance. The famed explorer Ferdinand Magellan, who was born in Portugal around 1480 and was the first to circumnavigate the globe, was a soldier at the Battle of Azemmour.[40]

The city of Azemmour has beautiful beaches, a great place for surfing, boogie boarding and kite sailing. The sand is fine and white in color, and the area is also known to locals as *Haouzia*. The area is also known for its pine trees and eucalyptus. Up the coast from Azemmour is the historic *Sidi Boubeker*, a famous lighthouse. It is situated on the coast in a town by the same name in the Jerada province of Oriental Morocco. The population of the town is about forty thousand, and it makes most of its income through tourism.[41] The lighthouse is about five miles up the coast of Morocco.

The *Medinah*, the Arabic word for "city," is the oldest portion of Azemmour. It contains the kasbah, or "castle," built by the Portuguese in the sixteenth century. One can still see its six towers and original cannons and the walls and ramparts of the Medinah. The castle also has the ruins of a prison and its two medieval towers. The most significant structure is the *Dar El Baroud* tower, which is all that remains of where the Portuguese gunpowder was stored.[42]

The Medinah also contained the Jewish sector of the city, about which we have spoken earlier in this first section. The remains of the Medinah also contain the mosque that predated the kasbah. In addition to these historical considerations, the city of Azemmour also is known for its religious significance, for it is known in Islam as a destination for many religious pilgrims.

Many Moroccan devotees visit the "Three Saints," whose temples are located in Azemmour. These are Moulay Bouchaib Erredad, Lalla

Aicha Bahriya, who is the saint of fertility, and Sidi Ouadoud, the patron saint of pottery. In order to venerate these saints, Moroccans from all over the country—both Muslims and Christians—travel to Azemmour to visit these shrines.[43]

Finally, one other fact about background information on the life of Estevanico of Morocco is that on January 2, 1492, the crown of Spain also banished all Muslims from their kingdoms. Like the Jews, these followers of the faith of Muhammad either converted to Roman Catholicism or they were banished—their only two options.

Earlier, in 1238, the Christian Reconquest had forced Spanish Muslims south, and the kingdom of Granada was established as the last refuge of the Moorish civilization in Spain. Granada flourished both culturally and economically for the next two hundred years. But in the late fifteenth century, internal feuds and a stronger Spanish monarchy under Ferdinand and Isabella began the end of Islam in Spain.

In 1502, the Spanish Crown ordered all Muslims to convert or leave Spain. The seventeenth century saw the continuation of persecutions against the Moors, and in 1609, the final remnant of those who practiced the faith of Muhammad was expelled permanently from Spain.

This brings us to the third section of this Introductory Essay on the life of Estevanico, in which we will explore the birth and early life of the famous Moroccan explorer, the first Black man in what will become the United States and Mexico.

## The Birth and Life of Estevanico

Very little is known of the life of Estevanico of Morocco. What we can be sure about the great explorer's early life, and can be documented, are seven or eight different aspects of his early life. The first of these is that he appears to have been born in the city of Azemmour, Morocco, either in 1500 or sometime around that year.[44]

The only available source that provides information about the early life of Estevanico is Helen Rand Parish's 1974 biography, *Estebanico*.[45] Parish gives the Moroccan slave's birth year as 1501, a year later than most other scholars. Parish also suggests that Estevanico's mother died a few months after his birth and that he was then cared for by a slave cook.[46]

Parish's biography also suggested that Estevanico was an errand boy, running among the port at Azemmour on the Moroccan coast, to the *Souk*, or "market" in Arabic, to the houses of merchants, and back to the shipping wharves in the city.[47] Parish said that at the age of eleven, Estevanico began learning his father's trade of iron-worker. She also maintained that Estevanico's parents were members of the North African Hausa Tribe, which would explain why our hero was said to be tall, large and powerful.[48]

A second fact we know about Estevanico, is that it is most likely that Estevanico was a Muslim at birth and thirdly, that he probably spoke Arabic at home as that was the chief language of the city at the time. Fourthly, given that he had a Christian name, he most likely was baptized at the time he became a slave in the year 1513. We will say more about this event next in this section of this study on the life of Estevanico.[49]

This baptism and conversion were most likely bestowed on the slave before he was added to the roster of the famous Narváez expedition that began in 1527 by Spanish explorer Pánfilo de Narváez (1470–1528).

It is also likely that Estevanico's original name was *Mustapha di Azemmour,* for "Mustapha" is the Arabic equivalent of the Christian name "Stephen." And in sixteenth-century Morocco, people were identified in terms of where they were from. The idea of having a "surname" did not enter Western Arabic culture until the nineteenth century.

Another thing we know about Estevanico's early life is that it was most probable that the young Moroccan was sold by the Portuguese to the Spaniard Narváez in Azemmour in 1513. At the time, Estevanico would have been somewhere between the ages of twelve and fifteen. Fifth, we know that the color of Estevanico's skin was dark enough that he was sometimes called "Stephen the Black," which may suggest that some of his ancestors may have been sub-Saharan.

With a crew of six hundred people, the goal of Narváez's 1527 exploratory mission was to create a permanent presence for the crown of Spain in the territory that was called "La Florida." Hispaniola (today, the Dominican Republic and Haiti) is an island in the Caribbean that is part of the Greater Antilles. It remains the most populated island in the West Indies, after the island of Cuba.

On the way to Hispaniola, however, the expedition experienced very bad weather, as well as attacks from local Native Americans. The weather was so bad that of the crew of six hundred, only four men survived the voyage to the New World. These men were Estevanico, Álvar Núñez Cabeza de Vaca, Andrés Dorantes de Carranza, and Alonso del Castillo Maldonado. These four men survived because they slowly sailed around the Gulf of Mexico. To achieve their goal, they needed to serve as slaves to the Native Americans, eventually reaching Spanish territory in modern-day Mexico.

After arriving safely, the other three Spanish explorers returned to Europe, while at the same time, Estevanico was sold a second time to Antonio de Mendoza, the Viceroy of New Spain.[50] Mendoza (1490–1552) was a viceroy in Mexico and then later in Peru. He was born in Granada into one of the oldest families in Spain. Mendoza entered into the service of Emperor Charles V, for whom he also served as a diplomat in Italy. Mendoza was appointed to be the first viceroy of New Spain in the New World when he arrived there in 1535.

According to the only available records from that time, Mendoza proved to be a prudent, firm and hard-working leader. He had the difficult task of consolidating the royal authority, correcting the abuses of tyrannical officials on the ground, and completing the pacification and conversion of the conquered Native Americans. At the same time, Mendoza was also in the business of making money to the maximum advantage of the Royal treasury of Spain.[51]

After fifteen years of being in charge of New Spain, Mendoza requested to return to Spain, where he wished to end his days. The crown refused his request, and instead, he was sent to Peru to consolidate the royal authority after a civil war among the conquistadores. One of his first acts in Peru was to send his son to examine the natives working in the mines. The viceroy of Peru fell ill, however, before he could improve the conditions in the mines.[52]

Antonio de Mendoza, ca. 1534.
Courtesy of Index Fototeca / Bridgeman Image

A full-length biography of Antonio Mendoza was completed in 1927 by Arthur Scott Aiton, of the history department at the University of Michigan, entitled *Antonio de Mendoza: First Viceroy of New Spain*.[53] Other subsequent works were written in 1966 and 1970, such as *The Spanish Seaborne Empire* by J. H. Parry and *The Conquest of the Incas* by John Hemming.[54]

One thing to add regarding Mendoza is that it was said he listened to the tales about the four survivors of the Narváez expedition and their belief that gold may be found further north. Thus, Mendoza organized a new exploration party led by Marcos de Niza (1500–1558), a French Franciscan friar. The main task of de Niza's expedition was to find the legendary "Seven Cities of Gold."[55]

During Marcos de Niza's expedition, Estevanico the Moroccan, or "Black Stephen," as the friar called him, served as the leading scout or guide for the Spanish exploratory party. Sadly, during de Niza's expedition, Estevanico was killed during one of his forays into North America. In fact, he was killed by the indigenous people of Hawikuh in their village of Zuni.[56]

Some say that Estevanico was killed because he was mistaken for an envoy of war because of his black skin. But for whatever reason, Estevanico was murdered at the hands of the Zuni warriors. After learning the fate of their scout, the expedition leader, Marcos de Niza, turned his group around and returned to the spot in present-day New Mexico from which they had come. This brings us to section four of this Introductory Essay on the life of black Moroccan explorer Estevanico, in which we will describe and discuss the other scouting parties conducted by him before he was murdered by the Zunis.

## Estevanico's Other Scouting Missions

We will begin this section on the life of Estevanico of Morocco with a summary of his travels from the time he sailed with the Spanish to the New World in 1527 until his death at the hands of the Zuni Native Americans in 1539. The timeline looks like this:

| Date | Mission/Activity |
|---|---|
| June 1527 | Travels to New World (Narváez Expedition). Lands on Hispaniola then Cuba. |
| April 1, 1528 | Reaches Tampa Bay, then Mississippi; Galveston, Texas; and the Rio Grande. |
| May 1, 1528 | Begins to explore Mexico. |
| July 1528 | Captured by Coahuiltecan Natives. |
| September 28, 1528 | Survivors embark on five poorly constructed boats. Estevanico in boat 3. |

| November 6, 1528 | Only one boat remains afloat. Estevanico is on it. |
|---|---|
| Fall 1530 | San Antonio Bay. |
| 1533 | Enters Mexico City. |
| Spring 1535 | To Arizona and New Mexico. |
| Winter 1536 | He lives among the Avavares Indians. |
| March 1536 | Meets a party of Spaniards there. Enters the Mexican state of Chiuahu. |
| February 1536 | Four explorers found in New Spain. |
| Autumn 1538 | Travels to Culiacán, Mexico. |
| March 7, 1539 | Left Mexico. |
| March 21, 1539 | De Niza sent Estevanico to scout the trail to the north. |
| May 1539 | Dies in Cibola, New Mexico (Zuni Country). Thirty miles south of Gallup, New Mexico. |
| 1540–1541 | Coronado returns to Cibola, which he called "Cevola" in his journal. |

In the remainder of this section, we will make several observations about many of the items on the timeline of Estevanico of Morocco, beginning with the Narváez expedition and the arrival in Hispaniola. One thing to remember, however, is that the traveling Estevanico and his comrades did in North America was all by foot. They walked thousands of miles from Florida to Texas, to Mexico, and then on to what would become the United States between 1527 and 1539, the year of Estevanico's death.

We know that the Narváez expedition left Spain in June of 1527. After stopping in Hispaniola, Haiti and the Dominican Republic, the expedition continued on to Cuba and then near present-day Tampa Bay, Florida. Narváez and his men were plagued by bad weather and a shortage of food.

Along for the voyage was Álvar Núñez Cabeza de Vaca, a Spaniard nobleman born in Jerez de la Frontera, Spain. De Vaca's early career was mostly in the military. In 1527, he was appointed to be the second in command of the expedition headed up by Pánfilo de Narváez, who wanted to claim the territory he found for the crown of Spain. Narváez's forces made their way north and then west along the southern coast of Florida to the Gulf of Mexico and Florida's panhandle.

Álvar Núñez Cabeza de Vaca. Courtesy of
Photo © Fonollosa/AIC/Bridgeman Images.

There, Narváez's army built five boats and then sailed haltingly along the coast of Alabama, Mississippi, Louisiana, and Texas. Three of the boats were lost, along with many of Narváez's soldiers, including Captain Narváez himself. The other explorers landed only to die of starvation or at the hands of the Native Indians.

Señor Cabeza de Vaca survived, as well as a few of his companions, including Estevanico. They finally landed off the coast of Texas on an island they called, "The Island of Misfortune." Later, this will be known as Galveston Bay. From 1529 until 1534, de Vaca and his companions lived a meager life among the Karankawa Indians.

The Karankawa were a group of tribes who lived along the Gulf of Mexico in what today is Texas. From archeological finds, we can be certain that the Karankawa can be traced back to at least the time of Christ. These tribes were nomadic and existed from Galveston Bay to Corpus Christi and as far inland as one hundred miles or so. For much of the eighteenth century, the Karankawa were at war with the Spaniards in Texas. They fought hard to retain their land, but by the beginning of the Civil War, the Karankawa were believed to be extinct.[57]

During this time in Texas, de Vaca and Estevanico began to exhibit their slight medical skills to the Indians as if they were confident medicine men. They often traveled with a special "Healing Gourd" that they frequently sent ahead of their arrival.

In 1534, Cabeza de Vaca and the other Spanish survivors—there were only four of them by then, including Estevanico, the other two being Alfonso de Castillo and Andrés Dorantes de Carranza—started to travel west in the direction of Texas and Mexico. With the help of many Native Americans along the way, they crossed the Pecos and then the Colorado Rivers. And made their way to Spanish outposts by 1536.[58]

Despite this arduous trip, Cabeza de Vaca continued to note his observations in his journal entitled the *Relación*.[59] Finally, they turned south and began to move inland, at first in Texas and then west to the Rio Grande River. Then the party went west again, and on the southern border of New Mexico, they moved into the interior of Mexico.[60]

By early April 1536, a slaving party from Spain found our four explorers, including Estevanico of Morocco. Soon after that—as our timeline suggests—Cabeza de Vaca was now in Mexico City. He stayed there for a while and then headed back to Spain in early 1537.[61]

Later, de Vaca led a second expedition in the New World in 1541 and 1542. His home base this time was Santos, Brazil. The trip began there and ended in Asuncion, Paraguay. In Paraguay, de Vaca was appointed governor of the Rio de la Plata. But a rebellion of his men seized power from him, and in 1545, de Vaca was forced again to return to Spain.[62] When he arrived back in Spain, he was arrested and charged with malfeasance in office, was convicted, and he died in shame. Among the extant evidence for Estevanico is a document that transfers ownership of "one Moroccan-born slave" to Viceroy Antonio de Mendoza, who in turn delivered the title to the Franciscan friar, Marcos de Niza. The price for the title is given in the document as "twelve silver Pesados."[63]

Meanwhile, when Estevanico left the service of de Vaca, the scout continued his work now under the direction of the Franciscan friar named Fray Marcos de Niza. The viceroy of Mexico in Mexico City, Antonio de Mendoza, was eager to hear the stories of the three remaining travelers. The viceroy asked the three explorers to lead another expedition, this time north to present-day Arizona and New Mexico.[64]

All but Estevanico of Morocco refused the assignment. In fact, Castillo and Dorantes decided to settle in Mexico, and both found wives. Estevanico, on the other hand, was game to help the viceroy and the friar. So, in February of 1539, the Moroccan led a small reconnaissance party on foot northward from Culiacán, Mexico, to Arizona and then into the northwest corner of New Mexico, where Estevanico died.[65]

As he had with many of the Indian villages that the scout visited, he sent ahead his "Magical Gourd" to the village of Cibola, which was supposed to be the first of the Seven Cities of Gold. While on his scouting mission, the Moroccan sent runners back daily to tell Fray de Niza how successful he had become. The plan was to send daily crosses that differed in size depending on the size of the progress that was made.[66] The crosses grew bigger and bigger each day.[67]

This brings us to section five of this Introductory Essay on the life of Estevanico of Morocco, in which we will describe and then discuss the death of our hero, the guide, explorer, linguist, and the first Black man in the United States.

## The Death of Estevanico

As our timeline indicates, on March 21, 1539, Fray Marcos de Niza sent his scout, Estevanico, northward to the village of Cibola in the northwestern corner of present-day New Mexico. At the time, the pueblo was known as *Hawikuh* and was populated since the early 1400s by Zuni Indians. This Zuni pueblo was the largest of the tribe's villages and the first to be seen by Europeans, in this case by the African Estevanico in the service of Spain.[68]

There are things we can be certain of regarding Estevanico's death, and there are also some questions that remain about his demise. For example, why did the Zuni chief order the Black man to be executed?

Among the aspects we can be certain of are the following:

1.  The Moroccan was sent north to visit the Seven Cities of Gold, of which Cibola/Hakiwuh was the first (March 21, 1539).
2.  Two Indian guides reported back to Fray Marcos de Niza that Estevanico had been murdered by the Zuni Indians.
3.  If the first Black slave in the United States was buried, we have no idea where his grave is now.

The items we cannot be sure of regarding the death of Estevanico the Moroccan are:

1.  Reports that the slave sent his "Magical Gourd" ahead to the village, and the chief is said to have smashed it.
2.  The same report continues that Estevanico was housed in a small hut outside the village for a few days.
3.  The same tradition relates that after three days, the Moroccan was struck by several arrows and killed.
4.  The Zunis also were said to memorialize the first Black man in America by fashioning a "black ogre kachina," a doll measuring about a foot tall that had protruding teeth, a black goatee, and black facial paint, which the Zunis called "*Chakwaina kachina*."[69]
5.  Another tradition has it that the body of Estevanico was chopped into several pieces and then eaten by the chieftains and elders of the Zuni people of the Southwest.

We will pause for a few comments in regard to the practices mentioned in items four and five in the above analysis. The great cultural anthropologist Sir James Frazer, in the volumes of his classic work the *Golden Bough*, pointed out that pre-literate human societies often employed two manners of thinking that are not generally used in modern, rational thinking.

Frazer called these the "Law of Similarity" and the "Law of Contagion." Together, these are sometimes called by anthropologists the "Laws of Sympathetic Magic." The first of these principles, Frazer tells us, is that "Like things produce like consequences." The second law, Frazer observes, "Once there is a causal connection between two things, that connection will remain forever."[70]

The Zuni Indians did make a black kachina to represent the body of Estevanico. This was following the law of similarity. If one then destroys the doll, it is like destroying the Black man. The chopping of the body of Estevanico into chunks and then being eaten by the tribe elders, the law of similarity thinking goes something like this: If X had a gift or skill, and we eat X's body, then we now inherit that skill.[71]

Similarly, when Estevanico had some commerce and communication with the Karankawa Tribe, many scholars complained about them being "cannibals," when in fact, all they were doing was practicing James Frazer's Law of Contagion, believing that the power of the warriors whose bodies they consume had become part of the power of the Karankawa, as well.

Now, this raises the question of what skill or skills did the Black Moroccan slave have that the Zuni Tribe elders wanted to emulate? We cannot be sure about the answer to that question, but spending considerable time with Estevanico most probably showed one of his skills for which he was well-known. That is, his facility and comfort with many different languages and dialects. In fact, it is likely that in the short time that the first Black man in America spent with the Zuni Indians, the elders must have noticed that he had begun to understand their language.

Needless to say, he must have done the same thing when he was forced to give up his native Arabic and replace it with Portuguese and then Castillian Spanish. Similarly, when Estevanico lived among the

Karankawa people, in a very short time, he had learned their language or at least the dialect that they spoke on the coast of Texas at the time, near Galveston Bay.

When French explorer Sieur de La Salle settled in Matagorda Bay in 1685, the number of Karankawa was estimated at four hundred men.[72] One of de La Salle's men, Henri Joutel, wrote a diary about his time with the Karankawa and one of the things he mentioned several times that he learned from the native people, is that "There was once a large, Black man who came to their land and quickly was able to communicate in the Karankawa language."[73]

The facility that Estevanico had for the understanding of and the ability to communicate in languages that were not his own was, undoubtedly, not the only skill of the first Black man in America that the Zuni Indians wished to acquire through their belief in Sympathetic Magic. The other skills are only to be guessed at but are not confirmed.

It is the case, however, for those who knew the Black Moroccan slave and who also wrote histories or narratives about him, the penchant that Estevanico had for languages was always part of those histories, diaries and narratives.

In fact, there is sufficient evidence that Estevanico learned some dialects of the Zuni, the tribe who murdered him; the Avavares, Plains Indians of the Great West whom he lived with for a while; and the Karankawa language he became fluent in, at least according to some of his biographers. Estevanico, and the Spanish in general, had friendly contacts with the Apache, who were called the *Querrecho*, along the Texas Panhandle in the early sixteenth century.[74]

In short, then, the Moroccan slave Estevanico was killed by Native Americans in a pueblo called Hawikuh, but he and his team called "Cibola," one of the supposed Seven Cities of Gold. He was murdered with bows and arrows by members of the Zuni Tribe of Arizona, New Mexico, and elsewhere in the Great West of America.

If we count his native Arabic, Portuguese and Spanish, with the addition of these Native American tongues, it is likely that Estevanico could communicate quite well in at least seven languages and maybe more.

Three other ways that the Zuni Indians may have employed the Laws of Similarity and Contagion regarding Estevanico had to do with his Black color and "Magical Gourd." His ability to heal, as well as his skills in the wilderness. The latter two of these aspects of Estevanico—like his ability in languages—are obvious. But the Black color and his healing gourd warrants more discussion.

The "Magical Gourd" carried by Estevanico and employed for healing was trimmed with owl feathers. The owl, because of its nocturnal life, was believed to be a symbol of death among the Zuni Indians. The skill of conjuring death may have been reinforced by the Black color of his skin.

The minds of the Zunis—which were susceptible to the Laws of Similarity and Contagion—made it easier for the Zuni Indians to believe that Estevanico's association with death was easily transferable by consuming his body parts after he was killed. Similarly, the Moroccan's skill of surviving in the wilderness, often alone or with a small scouting party, must have been admired, and desired, by the Zuni at the pueblo Hawikuh.

There is disagreement in the extant record about why the Zuni tribal members executed Estevanico. One elder told a researcher that the Moroccan guide had told them that a powerful army was "coming behind him with many weapons."[75] The elders are said to have met in council and decided that the Black man was a spy and that it was probably best to kill him.[76]

Once Estevanico was murdered, the Pueblo elders—as we have mentioned earlier—ordered that the Black man's body be cut up into small pieces that were then distributed to the elders to be consumed, an application of Fraser's Law of Contagion.

A year after the death of Estevanico, explorer Coronado visited Hawikuh, or Cibola, in July 1540. While his main army stayed at their base camp in Sonora, the advanced scout party occupied the pueblo of Hawikuh, and the Battle of Hawikuh ensued. On this same expedition, other scouts discovered the Grand Canyon, while others traveled to discover other pueblos along the Rio Grande River and the Great Plains full of Buffalo herds beyond.

Coronado Attacking Zuni-Cibola. *Landscape with an Episode from the Conquest of America*, ca.1535, oil on panel. Artist Jan Mostaert. Rijksmuseum, Amsterdam, The Netherlands. Courtesy of Bridgeman Images.

Francisco Vazquez de Coronado's (1510–1554) trip to Hawikuh and other sites in the great American West was important for many reasons. One of them for our purposes is that the Spanish explorer, when he arrived in Cibola/Hawikuh, was able to confirm many of the facts about the death of Estevanico, including that he was killed by bow and arrow and that his body parts were eaten by the Zuni elders.

The Cibola pueblo was conquered by Coronado in 1540. A mission church was built there named "La Purisima Concepcion" but was destroyed during the Great Pueblo Revolt of 1680 when the New Mexican pueblos rose up against the Spanish. The pueblo of Cibola, or Hawikuh, was permanently abandoned by the Zuni people just after the rebellion. At its peak, the primary compound of the pueblo had up to 150 rooms surrounded by a central plaza. The structure stood four levels high with multiple numbers of *kivas*, and great kivas, with a population of around seven hundred people. There are now extensive archeological ruins atop the long, narrow ridge where the pueblo existed, as well as the mission church.

A great *kiva* in the Zuni language was a large, circular and usually subterranean structure used by Pueblo Indians for important events such as religious ceremonies or important political gatherings. The "Great Kivas" are sometimes called the earliest examples of "public architecture" in the Americas. The larger kiva most often had more than 100 square meters of space.[77]

The Great Kiva at the Chaco Culture National
Historical Park in New Mexico.

Two other questions about the death of Estevanico remain. Why did the Zuni Indians decide to murder the Moroccan, and why did the Franciscan friar, de Niza, not continue on to Cibola/Hawikuh as he had planned? Instead, after getting word of the death of Estevanico, the friar immediately returned to Mexico City and then, a short time later, returned to Spain. Connected to this second question is another query. Why did de Niza decide to accompany Coronado on his 1540 trek to the Seven Cities of Gold, a year later?

This brings us to the sixth section of this Introductory Essay on the life of Estevanico, the first Black man in America, in which we will describe and discuss the many influences that the Moroccan slave had on others.

## The Influences of Estevanico

It should be clear that the two main places in Western and American history where Estevanico's influences may be seen are with subsequent explorers of the New World and in the history of slavery in the Western Hemisphere. We will deal with these two influences in reverse order.

There can be no doubt that Estevanico was sold into slavery somewhere between the ages of eleven and thirteen. When he traveled to the New World in 1527 with the Spanish voyage of Pánfilo de Narváez (1470–1528), the Moroccan is listed on the ship manifest as a "Negro" slave.[78]

While working as a scout for Andrés Dorantes de Carranza, the governor of New Spain, and Marcos de Niza, there can be no doubt that Estevanico was considered to be a slave in the employ of the Spanish Crown. In this sense, the Morrocan was not only the first Black man in what would become the continental United States, but he was also the first slave.

This is significant for many reasons, but one of the central of these is that Estevanico was a slave more than a century before 1619 when the organizers of the "1619 Project" of the *New York Times* suggested that slavery began in the United States in the year 1619, in Jamestown, Virginia.[79]

Over the next two hundred years, from 1619 to 1865, more than twelve million African slaves were brought to the Americas. But one interesting fact is that less than five hundred thousand of those captives were brought to what became the American Colonies or the United States.[80] At any rate, there are documents extant that suggest that Estevanico was given his freedom in 1536, and it was as a free man that he accompanied the expedition led by Fray Marcos de Niza to the Seven Cities of Gold in western New Mexico.

In this sense, then, the "1619 Project," perhaps, should be renamed the "1513 Project" because it was in that year that the Portuguese bought Estevanico and subsequently sold him into slavery under the

Spanish Crown. Estevanico was enslaved in 1513 and remained that way until three years before his death in 1539.

As suggested earlier, the other place where the influence of Estevanico can be seen most clearly is in subsequent New World explorers that came after the time of the slave from Morocco.

Already in this Introductory Essay, we have spoken of the influence that Estevanico had on the discoveries of Francisco Vásquez de Coronado, who, among other things, continued the slave from Morocco's exploration of the southwest of North America in 1540, the year after Estevanico's death. We also discussed the role of Fray Marcos de Niza, the Franciscan friar who also is said to have explored the fabled Seven Cities of Gold in what is now the western portion of New Mexico.

These two Spanish gentlemen can be tied directly to the influence of "Little Stephen," or Estevanico. But there are also some that the slave from Morocco influenced indirectly, such as Hernando de Soto, Sebastian Cabot and Jacques Cartier, for example, in a list of dozens of explorers. We picked these three because they come from different nations—Spain, England and France.

Hernando de Soto (1500–1542) was a Spanish explorer, who despite having a new wife and home in Spain, grew restless when he heard stories about Cabeza de Vaca's explorations of Florida and the Gulf Coast. De Soto is said to have sold all his belongings and financed his own voyages on ten ships and a crew of seven hundred. From April 1538 until May 1542, de Soto explored what today would be Georgia and Alabama and then later crossed the Mississippi River, where he died of a fever on May 21, 1542.[81] Estevanico only indirectly influenced de Soto because the latter heard stories about the former and then wished to go explore for himself. By the time he died, more than half his men had died by disease or in battles against the Native Americans.[82]

Although he was born in Italy, Sebastian Cabot sailed for the British Crown to the New World.[83] In fact, he continued the work of his father, who was also an explorer. Like Estevanico, Sebastian Cabot fell under the mystery of the quest for gold in the New World. Many of his treks were near Hudson Bay in Canada, along with Newfoundland, and he mapped these areas for future British explorations. Cabot would also explore Central and South America. Later, he gave up his service to the crown of Britain and began expeditions for Spain instead.

Believing he had discovered El Dorado, a friar erected
a cross to claim the shining city then fled.
Courtesy of Look and Learn / Bridgeman Images.

Another similarity between Estevanico and Sebastian Cabot is a kind of spirit of wanderlust and abandonment that took both men to great discoveries. At the very end of Cabot's life in 1547, he returned to the employ of the British to work for the young King Edward VI. Cabot was given the title "Great Navigator" as he updated the British maps of the New World. He also became an advisor to various expeditions looking for what was called the "Northeast Passage" by way of Russia. Sebastian Cabot also became the lifetime director of the "Company of Merchant Adventurers," an organization of which, if Estevanico was not murdered in 1539, he could very well have gone on to be a member.

Finally, Jacques Cartier, a French navigator and explorer, has been credited with the naming of Canada, exploring the Saint Lawrence River, as well as many areas that would become French territory. Although Cartier named the land he traveled in "Canada," the word actually comes from the Iroquois-Huron languages. These native Americans referred to the village of Stacona, or Stadacona, as *Kanata*.[84] If there is any direct, or indirect influence on Cartier from the life of slave, Estevanico, it is the importance of learning Native American languages to better understand the natives as both Estevanico and Cartier had done.

This brings us to Chapter One, in which we will identify and discuss several pieces of background information for helping to understand the life of Estevanico, the first Black man in America.

# I
# The Birth and Background of Estevanico

The word "Negro" has become a very sensitive term, loaded
with negative connotations. Whatever its original meaning, a
specific race of Africans or just black-skinned people of
general African descent, that meaning has deteriorated in the
popular imagination. It is not surprising that many Blacks, particularly in North America, now react to the word with varying
degrees of pain and disgust.

—Ivan Van Sertima, *They Came Before Columbus*

We will begin these remarks with what the historical record can tell us
about the birth, early life and background of Estevanico. It is likely that
he was born sometime between 1500 and 1503 in Azemmour, Morocco.
It is also probable that his family was Muslim and that he spoke Arabic
at home, for it was his first language.

The name of the tribe from which Estevanico belonged was
*Doukkali* since this is the name of the people to which most people in
Azemmour and al-Jadida were members. Estevanico's Moorish origin
and dark complexion suggest that Estevanico may have had some
Black ancestors farther south of the Sahara Desert, but we cannot be
certain about this.

Little else is known about the early life of our Moroccan hero.
We do know, however, that Portugal took control of Morocco in 1513
and that they brought Estevanico most likely to Seville, Spain, to be
sold into slavery. In fact, it appears that in 1522, when Estevanico
was in his early twenties, he was sold to a Spanish nobleman named

Andrés Dorantes de Carranza. In fact, we are certain that Estevanico was enslaved sometime after 1513 at a very early age and then brought to Seville, Spain, where he was purchased around 1522 by Spaniard de Carranza, who took the Moroccan slave along in the 1527 expedition of Pánfilo de Narváez that arrived in North America in September of 1528.

We know that at the time, Spain did not allow non-Roman Catholics—particularly Jews and Muslims—to travel to the New World. So, it is likely that Estevanico was required to convert to Roman Catholicism for him to join his master and the expedition of Narváez to the New World. The Moroccan slave's Christian name was *Esteven* or "Stephen" in Portuguese. The moniker "Estevanico" is a diminutive form of the name Stephen.

One other fact that is undeniable is that by the age of twenty-five, the Moroccan slave known as Estevanico already had a mastery and comfort in three different languages—Classical Arabic, Portuguese and Castillian Spanish. But there are several other pieces of background information about the life of our Morocco hero, and we will turn next to these in the second chapter of this narrative of the life of Estevanico, the first Black man in America, in which we will speak of Estevanico as a Muslim.

# II
# Estevanico as a Muslim

It is likely that Estebanico's faith was the religion of the Prophet
Muhammad, Islam, and that the language that was his first was
the Classical Arabic spoken in his native city of Azemmour of
Morocco, in North Africa.

—Helen Rand Parish, *Estebanico*

In addition to the background information, we will also provide some observations that we have simply labeled here, "Estevanico as a Muslim."

After Islam began in the Arabian Peninsula in the seventh century CE, it quickly expanded throughout Arabia and then across North Africa, including the home of our hero in Azemmour, Morocco, by the second half of the seventh century CE.

After North Africa, Islam spread throughout much of West Africa by way of merchant traders, scholars and missionaries, largely by peaceful means, whereby many African rulers either prosecuted the faith of Muhammad or converted to it themselves. In this way, Islam spread across and around the Sahara Desert. Meanwhile, Islam entered East Africa when Arab traders crossed the Red Sea and then, in a second wave, made excursions along the Swahili coast.

Meanwhile, back in Morocco, the land went through a series of Islamic dynasties, beginning with a consolidation of Berber kingdoms from 744 to 1058, known as the *Barghawata* dynasty. The *Almoravid* dynasty came next from 1160 to 1147, followed by the *Almohads* from 1121 to 1269. These Moroccan dynasties were followed by the Marinids from 1270 until 1465.[85]

The Moroccan dynasty in charge when Estevanico was born in Azemmour between 1500 and 1503, was known as the *Wattasid* dynasty that lasted from 1472 until 1554. The Wattasid leaders promised the Moroccan people that they would protect them from foreign incursions. By the first years of the sixteenth century, the Portuguese had increased their presence on the coast of Morocco.

By 1513, the Portuguese invaded the portion of Morocco at Azemmour and surrounding areas. Among their other activities there, Portugal captured a number of Muslim Moroccans who spoke Classical Arabic, including our hero, Estevanico. The Portuguese made other strongholds on the coast, including Tangiers, Ceuta and Maziyen.

There can be little doubt that Estevanico's native tongue was Arabic, as it was for everyone else living in and around Azemmour at the beginning of the sixteenth century. In the south of Morocco, a new dynasty began to emerge called the *Saadian* dynasty that seized the city of Marrakesh in 1524. Indeed, they made the city their capital.

It is also likely in these early years of Estevanico's life, he learned and practiced the most fundamental beliefs of Islam. These include:

1. Belief in the Oneness of Allah (Tawhid)
2. Belief in Angels (mala'ika)
3. Belief in the Books of God, the Bible and Al-Qur'an (Kitub)
4. Belief in the Prophet Muhammad as a Messenger of Allah (Nubuwwah)
5. Belief in the Day of Judgment (Ma'ad or Yom Qiamah)
6. Belief in Divine Decree (Qadar)

In addition to these fundamental beliefs, the observant Muslim in early sixteenth-century Morocco also would have adhered to a code of religious obligations. These are sometimes called the "Five Pillars of Islam," which include the following:

1. Shahadah, "Profession of Faith."
2. Salat, or the obligation to pray five times a day.
3. Zakat, or the giving of alms.
4. Ramadan, or observing a month-long yearly fast.

5.  Hajj, or a pilgrimage to the Holy City of Mecca and to the Ka'bah cubical structure in the center of Mecca.[86]

If Estevanico and his family were truly observant members of the Islamic faith, they would have been required to have met these five religious obligations, as well as the six fundamental beliefs mentioned above. Thus, we should add the moniker "First Muslim Man in America" to our list of many "firsts" regarding the Moroccan slave Estevanico.

## Estevanico as a Berber

Another way that Estevanico may be identified is simply to say he was a Berber, or what they call themselves in Morocco, the *Wattasids*, or *Banu Wattas*, in classical Arabic. The Berber people also identify themselves as the *Amazigh*, or even the *Imazighen*, another name for the Berber languages.

The Berbers are an ethnic group indigenous to the Maghreb region of North Africa, where they still live in scattered communities across parts of Morocco, Algeria and Libya, and to a lesser extent in Tunisia, Mauritania, and the northern parts of Mali and Niger. Smaller Berber communities can also be found in Egypt's Siwa Oasis. Historically, Berber people have spoken Berber languages, which are a group of the larger Afro-Asiatic language family.

In a very real way, it is appropriate to say that the hero of this study, Estevanico of Azemmour, could be considered an individual of the Berber People, whether his family spoke any of the Berber languages or not.

At the time of the birth of Estevanico, around 1500, there were two official languages in Morocco. These were standard classical Arabic and the standard Moroccan Berber language. The former was the standard common speech in sixteenth-century Morocco, but the latter served—and continues to serve—a significant part of the country's vernacular. It is likely, therefore, that our hero Estevanico was familiar with a number of Berber words and expressions that had entered into the common talk of Moroccans at the beginning of the sixteenth century.

Since the early sixteenth century, about 90 to 95 percent of all Berbers spoke one or more of seven Berber languages. These are

Tachelhit, Kabyle, Tamazight, Riffian, Shawiya, and Tuareq. An eight Berber language known as Guanche is now extinct. Guanche was mostly spoken on the Canary Islands and now can only be found in southern Egypt and northern Sudan.

Today, because Morocco was a French colony, the second language for about a third of all Moroccans is French, but that would be much too late for our hero from Azemmour. French is also the official language in Moroccan universities, as well as in economics, medicine, education and in government institutions.

No scholar to our knowledge has written about the places that Berber culture and the Berber languages and dialects have played in the childhood of Estevanico of Azemmour. We suspect, however, that a significant number of Berber words and expressions had seeped into the language of the common man, or person, in early sixteenth-century Morocco. Thus, we would be prudent to add the language, or languages of the *Banu Wattas*, to the list of the tongues about which Estevanico was familiar or had mastered.

This brings us to Chapter Three of this study on the life of Estevanico, where we will explore the Moorish background of Estevanico. This will be followed by Chapter Four, which includes additional background information that will be very helpful in understanding the life and times of the Moroccan slave Estevanico of Azemmour.

# III
# Estevanico as a Moor

Estevanico of Azamor, a Moorish Muslim, began exploring
America in the 16th century. He landed in Florida in 1527 and
until 1539, explored Arizona and New Mexico.

—Ibn Masud, "History of Islam in the Americas,"
*Sunnah Muakada*[87]

Christian Europeans first employed the noun "Moor" and the adjective
"Moorish" to designate the Muslim inhabitants of the Maghreb, or
the Iberian Peninsula, certain portions of Sicily and Malta during the
Middle Ages. The Moors originally were indigenous Berber people.
The name and adjective were later applied to Arabs and Arabized
people of Iberia.

The Moors, then, were not a distinct nor self-defined people. The
1911 *Encyclopedia Britannica* pointed out that the word "Moor" "had
no real ethnological value."[88] Nevertheless, Christians of the Middle
Ages and the Early Modern period variously applied the name to Arabs,
North African Berbers, as well as Muslim Europeans. In this sense,
Estevanico was considered by many to be a Moor.

The word Moor was also used more generally in Europe to refer
to anyone of Arab or African descent and sometimes were known as
"Blackamoors." The word comes from the Classical Greek *mauros*,
whose plural is *mauroi*, meaning "black" or "very dark." In Latin, the
word became *Niger*, or even *fusco*, which also meant "very dark." It is
clear that both the Greeks and Romans saw the dark-skinned *Aithiops*

as a separate group of people. In fact, in the New Testament in Acts of the Apostles 8:27, the Koine Greek *aitho* or "to scorch" is employed to speak of scorching the face of an Ethiopian.[89]

In Arab literature, there is little reference to the words Moor and Moorish. Rather, cultural anthropologist Dana Reynolds suggests that the Berbers emerged as the result of the admixture of non-African and African, who moved into the Maghreb during the second millennium BCE.[90]

Saint Isidore of Seville (560–636) pointed out that the Greek *maurus* means "black." By the late fifteenth century, the Italian Roberto di San Severino makes a distinction between Moors and Arabs. In a trip to the Holy Land, Severino wrote about the latter's observance of their *Ramatana*, most likely a reference to "Ramadan" mentioned in the previous section of this study.[91]

Shortly before the birth of Estevanico in 1492, the Moor kingdom of Granada marked the end of Muslim control in Spain and Portugal, but a Muslim minority remained in Iberia until their final expulsion in 1609. Nevertheless, the cultural environment into which Estevanico was born included the Moors, who ruled Spain for eight hundred years and contributed great historical developments in the fields of science, mathematics, geography and philosophy.

One way to judge the effects that Moorish culture had on Spain is to ascertain the number of Arabic words and Arabic-derived phrases that were absorbed into modern Spanish. Some estimate as many as four thousand words and phrases. Among these words and phrases are:

- Algebra – Checkmate
- Alcohol – Influenza
- Chemistry – Typhoon
- Alkaline – Orange
- Lute – Cable
- Guitar – Cipher

Moorish culture also introduced many new crops to Europe and North Africa, including the orange, lemon, dates and pomegranate, as well as saffron, sugar cane, cotton, silk and rice.

In terms of cultural developments in the West, Moorish culture introduced the use of paper to Europe and the employment of Arabic numerals to replace Greco-Roman systems of numbering. They also, through the ninth-century musician *Ziryab*, or "Blackbird," also brought the earliest versions of several musical instruments to Europe, including the lute, or what they called *el oud*; the guitar, or *kithara*, in Arabic; and the lyre.

The Moorish culture from which Estevanico came also introduced a new style for consuming meals by converting large feasts into several courses that began with soup and ended with what we would call dessert.

The Moorish leaders lived in sumptuous palaces. One such palace was the Alhambra, literally the "Red One," in Granada, the Moorish stronghold and one of Spain's architectural masterpieces. Alhambra was the seat of Muslim rule in Spain from the thirteenth century to the fifteenth century.

The Moors also ruled and occupied what is today Lisbon but was called *Lashbuna* by the Moors. And that name was used for the city, and for Portugal in general, well into the twelfth century. The Moors were finally driven out by the forces of King Alfonso Henriques in what is now called the Battle of Castello de Sao Jorge, or the "Castle of Saint George."[92]

The Moorish influences in Iberia, however, were far from over. By 1500 and the time of the birth of Estevanico, the people of North Africa and the Iberian Peninsula were often still called "Moors." This was certainly true of our Moroccan slave from Azemmour, who, in the historical literature, is often called "Estevanico the Moor."

One final aspect of Moorish culture that had great influence in the West was the extraordinary level of scholarship among the Moors. One fine example is the Moor called Averroes in the West, whose Arabic name was Ahmad Ibn Rushd. Averroes lived in Cordoba among the Spanish Moors from 1126 to 1198.

Ibn Rushd was a universal and multi-talented scholar who worked in physics, astronomy, mathematics, philosophy and Koranic Studies, as well as being a physician. He also aided in keeping alive the Greek philosophical tradition of Aristotle, bringing it to the West.

In his drama *Othello*, William Shakespeare incorporates the idea of the Afro-European Moors, for the title character in the play is designated as a "Moor."

This brings us to Chapter Four of this study on the life and times of Estevanico, in which we will describe and discuss many other pieces of background information that are vital in understanding our Moroccan hero, the first Black man in America, Estevanico.

Abu l-Walid Muhammad bin 'Ahmad bin Rusd, better known as Ibn Rushd, and in European literature as Averroes. Bridgeman images.

# IV
# Background Information on Estevanico

He was born a Muslim, but because Spain did not allow
non-Catholics to travel to the New World, some historians
believe he converted to Roman Catholicism, though these claims
remain dubious. He was sold to Andrés Dorantes de Carranza, a
Spanish nobleman.

—Diego de Guzman, a contemporary of Estevanico

In this fourth chapter, we will describe and discuss several aspects of life in the Iberian Peninsula that will provide more background information on several aspects of life from the fourteenth century to the sixteenth century. Among those aspects are the following: the coming of Islam to Iberia, the coming of Judaism and its place in Iberian culture and religion, the Edict of Expulsion of 1492, the modern history of Morocco and particularly the city of Azemmour where Estevanico was born to an Arabic-speaking family, and a number of other aspects of life in Spain and Portugal from 1450 until 1539, the year of the death of Estevanico.

We will begin this discussion of background materials for the life and times of Estevanico, the first Black man in America, with some observations about the history of modern Morocco and the city of Azemmour, where our hero was born sometime between 1500 and 1503.

## Modern Morocco and Azemmour

The history of hominid occupation in Morocco goes back to the Lower Paleolithic age. Archeological evidence shows that the area was inhabited by humans at least four hundred thousand years ago. The recorded history of Morocco began with the Phoenicians with Morocco being colonized between the eighth and sixth century BCE.[93]

In the fifth century BCE, the city-state of Carthage extended its control over the coastal areas of North Africa. By the time of Christ, the Romans had control of Morocco. In the mid-fifth century CE, it was overthrown by the Vandals before it was recovered by the Byzantine Empire in the sixth century CE.[94]

Muslim armies conquered the region of North Africa and Morocco in the seventh and eighth centuries, but Morocco broke away from the Umayyad Caliphate after something called the "Berber Revolt" in 740 CE. It took place during the reign of Caliph Hisham ibn Abd al-Malik. This marked the first successful attempt to break away from the Arab Caliphate that ultimately was ruled by Damascus.[95] The Berber Revolt began in Tangiers and was initially led by Maysara al-Matshari.[96] The revolt quickly spread through the rest of the Maghreb, or North Africa, and then across the Strait of Gibraltar into what was known as *Al-Andalus*.[97]

The army of the Umayyad was scrambled, and it managed to prevent the regions of *Ifriqiya*, or Tunisia, Eastern Algeria, and Western Libya, along with Al-Andalus, or parts of Spain and Portugal, from falling into the Berber rebel control. After failing to capture the Umayyad, the provincial capital at the city of Kairouan, the Berber army dissolved, and the Western portion of the Iberian Peninsula was fragmented into a series of small Berber states ruled by imams and tribal chieftains.[98]

Many historians regard the Umayyad's response to the Berber Revolt as the beginning of the Moroccan independence, for Morocco would never again come under the rule of an eastern Caliph, or any other power for that matter, until the twentieth century.

With the decline of local Berber dynasties in the fifteenth and sixteenth centuries, the valuable coastal strip of North Africa, known because of the Berbers as the Barbary Coast, attracts the attention of the three great powers of the Mediterranean at the time, Portugal and Spain in the west, and Turkey in the east.

The rivalry between the Spanish and the Turks lasts for much of the sixteenth century, but it is gradually won in a somewhat unorthodox way by using Turkish pirates. The idea was that Turk corsairs or small ships would establish themselves along the coast of North Africa. The territories seized by these corsairs were then given a formal status as part of the Protectorate of the Ottoman Empire.

The first of these great pirates established himself on the coast of what is today Algeria in 1512. Two other pirates are firmly ensconced in Libya by 1551. Tunisia was briefly taken in 1534 by the most famous corsair pirate of them all, Khair ad-Din, better known to the Europeans as Barbarossa. Tunisia was recovered from Spain in 1535 and eventually brought to the Ottoman Empire in 1574.

The United States was involved in a series of wars with the Barbary pirates from 1801 to 1805 and 1815 to 1816. The Barbary states, many of which practiced state-supported piracy in order to exact tributes from weaker Atlantic powers, began to seize ships off the coast of North Africa. Even as early as 1785, Dey Muhammad of Algeria declared war on the United States and captured several of their vessels. This conflict continued for the next thirty years and ended after negotiations that ended on December 23, 1815. There was not a treaty between the United States and the Barbary states until February 11, 1822.

Piracy remained the chief purpose and main source of income for all these Turkish settlements along the Barbary Coast, and the depredations of piracy after three centuries, at last, prompted the French to intervene in its colony in Algeria that was initially occupied by the French in 1830, but it was only by 1847 that the French conquest of Algeria was complete.

The French received some resistance from the Berbers in the countryside and hinterlands, which had never been completely controlled by the Turks on the coast. Tunisia became a French Protectorate in 1881, and Morocco, which had been maintaining a shaky independence under its own sultans since the end of the Marinid dynasty, followed in 1912. Italy took Libya from the Turks in 1912. Thus, the region of the Barbary Coast was about to enter its last phase before independence.

By the beginning of the twentieth century, France and Spain began carving out zones of influence in North Africa. In 1884, Spain created a protectorate in the coastal areas of Morocco. By the fall of 1906, France and Spain agreed to police the ports of the Moroccan coast. They also agreed on collected customs fees and taxes. In 1912, Morocco became a French protectorate under something called the "Treaty of Fez," in which the country was ruled by a French resident-general who largely had a figurehead role.

From 1921 until 1926, tribes in the mountains began to rebel and were eventually suppressed by Spanish and French troops. Thirty years later, in March of 1956, the French protectorate in Morocco ended, although Spain kept its two coastal enclaves. A year later, in 1957, Sultan Mohammed became the king of Morocco.[99] However, he only ruled for four years. He died on February 26, 1961, due to complications related to surgery and was replaced by King Hassan II.[100]

As indicated earlier in the Introductory Essay of this study, Estevanico was born in the city of Azemmour sometime between 1500 and 1503. The city is located on the left bank of the Oum Er-Rbia River, the second-largest river in Morocco. For a short period of its urban history, Azemmour was under the control of the Portuguese from 1513 until 1541.

In fact, on August 28 and 29, 1513, the Portuguese did battle with what was called the Wattasid dynasty in what came to be called the "Battle of Azemmour."[101] Estevanico, who would have been thirteen or so at the time, may very well have been present at the battle. We also know at that time the Moroccan Estevanico was sold into slavery by the Portuguese to the Spaniards.[102]

Azemmour, Morocco, is 75 kilometers, or forty-seven miles, southwest of Casablanca. This city into which Estevanico was born between 1500 and 1503 was Arabic-speaking. At the time, the medieval city consisted of three main parts—a Jewish mellah, a kasbah, or castle, and the old Medina, or city. The historical lighthouse of Sidi Boubker is located eight kilometers, or five miles, north of Azemmour.

In addition to Estevanico, the most famous contemporary resident of Azemmour is probably Abdallah Laroui, born in 1933, a Moroccan historian, novelist and philosopher, but clearly, Estevanico is much better known than Laroui.

## Judaism in Azemmour and Morocco

This brings us to a discussion of the Jewish Mellah in Azemmour, our next topic of background information on Estevanico. As mentioned in the Introductory Essay of this study, Jews first arrived in Estevanico's Morocco in pre-Christian times when they accompanied the Phoenicians on their trade expeditions across the coast of Morocco. In the countryside, Jewish and Berber Tribes tended to the soil side by side together for two thousand years, speaking a Berber dialect of the Punic languages.[103]

In the Moroccan towns and cities, Jewish merchants and moneylenders were valued by successive generations of leaders of Morocco who protected the Jews. One of these leaders was King Mohammed VI, who inherited his father's penchant for tolerance toward the Jews. One of Mohammed VI's principal advisors was a Jewish man named Andre Azoulay, who had also served King Hassan II.[104]

As indicated earlier, a grant of privilege was conferred on the Jews in Morocco on June 14, 1514, that also fixed the tax rate for the Moroccan Jews. Two years before, Rabbi Joseph Adibe was appointed Rabbi of Azemmour. The community flourished in those days, and, as a child, Estevanico, or "Little Stephen," must have known and visited the Jewish *Mellah* in his hometown.

After the Portuguese control of Azemmour, beginning in 1513, the same year that Estevanico was sold into slavery to the Spanish Crown, the Moroccan slave would never see his homeland again. But until 1513, he surely was aware of the Jewish influences in his hometown.

Today Morocco's Jewish sites are located in Marrakech and Fez, mostly because these two Imperial cities have preserved the Jewish *Mellah*s in the Medinah, or "Old Cities." But other Jewish sites also can be found throughout Morocco. The majority of these sites are now in new cities or villages. It is still the case, however, that Jewish sites are protected by the Kingdom of Morocco.[105]

There are still many Jewish shrines and cemeteries in Morocco that are visited by Jewish pilgrims whose ancestors may have been Moroccan Jews. Near the city of Marrakech is the famous Jewish Zaouia of Telouet, which was once the seat of the French protectorate in Morocco. Some twenty miles from Marrakech is the tomb of Moulay Ighi, perched on a hilltop in the Atlas Mountains. It too is now a shrine visited by Muslims and Jews alike.[106]

The Rabbi Pinhas Synagogue remains the oldest Jewish house of worship in Morocco. It is on a street called the "Rue Talmud Torah." The synagogue was established in 1538 and is located next to a Jewish cemetery called "Miaara" with its sparking white tombs. The cemetery is much older than the synagogue, so it is likely that Estevanico visited the Jewish burial ground in his hometown prior to his abduction and sale into slavery—the next section of this first chapter of this study of "Little Stephen," or Estevanico. Before that, however, we will speak of two other pieces of background materials for this study of the life of Estevanico—The Muslim conquest of North Africa and the Edict of Expulsion from the year 1492.

## The Muslim Conquest of North Africa

As mentioned in the Introductory Essay that began this study, we suggested that the emergence of Islam in the seventh century CE and its spread to North Africa is another important aspect of background materials for the life of Estevanico. The Islamic prophet Muhammad died in 632 CE. Immediately after his death, the Muslim army began conquering much of what we think of today as the "Middle East." This included Persia, as well as much of North Africa, including parts of Spain and Portugal, across the Strait of Gibraltar, where the Atlantic Ocean meets the Mediterranean Sea.

By the year 670, nearly fifty years after the death of Muhammad, Arab general Oqbah ibn Nafi had founded the holy city of Kairouan in Tunisia. From there, and in 682, Oqba led his army all the way to the Atlantic coast of Morocco. He named this land "*Al Maghrib*," the Arabic name still used for the city by locals. The word *maghrib* in Classical Arabic means "the Far West."[107]

The prospect of an invasion of the rich Spanish and Portuguese peninsula made many Berbers convert to Islam, and many of them joined the Muslim Army to help carry the banner of Islam across the Mediterranean. For the next six centuries—from the eighth to the fifteenth century—the Islamic civilizations of Spain and Portugal were among the most sophisticated people in the world and outshone anything in Christian Europe from the same period.

To cite one example, during the period in question, the Islamic world in the history of philosophy produced Al-Ghazali, Al-Farabi, Ibn Rushd, Ibn Sina, and a host of other thinkers long before Thomas Aquinas in the thirteenth century.

From the time of the Muslim conquest in the seventh and eighth centuries to the formation of the French protectorate in Morocco in the twentieth century, the political history of North Africa was that of an uninterrupted series of Islamic dynasties. After consolidating power, subduing enemies and building monumental cities, mosques and even palaces, each successive regime came to power and then slid into decadence.

Indeed, most of these Muslim dynasties before the arrival of the French ended with weak governments, political chaos and bitter in-fighting until the new regime stepped up to rule Azemmour and Morocco.

From 647 until 800, the Arabs invaded North Africa in three separate invasions. The first from 647 to 664, the second from 665 until 689, and the third from 690 until 800. From then on, most of North Africa became Islamic both in culture and religion.

This brings us to the Expulsion of 1492, our final aspect of background information for understanding the life of Estevanico from Morocco, the first Black man in America, who arrived in what would become the United States in 1528, nearly a century before the *New York Times* "1619 Project," whose writers place the first Black men in America to the Virginia colony in 1619.

## The Edict of Expulsion

The Edict of Expulsion of 1492, also known as the "Alhambra Decree," was an edict jointly issued by the Catholic monarchs of Spain— Isabella I of Castile and Ferdinand II of Aragon—on March 31, 1492, expelling all Jews from territories belonging to the Spanish monarchs. The primary purpose of the edict appears to have been the elimination of any influence on Spanish society. It went so far that it forbade the practice of the Jewish faith anywhere in Spain.

The crowns of Spain gave all Jewish people in their realms three choices—convert, leave or be turned over to the Spanish Inquisition. By 1500, more than half of the Jews in Spain chose the first option. An estimated three hundred thousand Jews chose the second option, and many thousand other Jews were burned at the stake in what the Spanish, and later the Portuguese, would call an *Auto da Fe*, or an "Act of Faith." It is of some interest that the government did not formally revoke the Edict of Expulsion of the Jews in Spain until December 16, 1968.

Meanwhile, it was also in 1492 on January second of that year, when the Kingdom of Granada fell to the Christian Armies of King Ferdinand V and Queen Isabella I, at which time the Moors began to lose their foothold in Spain, as well.

The Kingdom of Granada was located at the confluence of the Darro and Genil Rivers in southern Spain. The city of Granada was built as a Moorish fortress that rose to prominence during the reign of Sultan Almoravid in the eleventh century. In 1238, the Christian re-conquest began to force Muslims south, and the Kingdom of Granada was established as the final refuge of the Moorish civilization.

Granada flourished both culturally and economically in the sixteenth and seventeenth centuries. In the late fifteenth century, however, internal feuds and the strong crown in Spain began to signal the end of Islam in Spain. In fact, on January 2, 1492, King Boabdil surrendered Granada to the Christian Spanish army.

Like the Jews of Spain, the Moors were given the same choices, convert to Catholicism or leave. By 1502, around the time that Estevanico was a toddler, the Spanish Crown ordered all Muslims to either be forcibly converted or leave Granada and Spain.

The Arabic speakers of North Africa had a special word for Muslims who falsely converted to Christianity in 1492 and afterward. That Arabic word was *taqiyah*, which comes from the Classical Arabic verb *waqa* meaning "to shield oneself," presumably in the sense of appearing as a false convert.

This brings us to Chapter Five of this study of the life of Estevanico from Morocco, the first Black man in America, his being sold into slavery, his conversion and finally, his coming to America.

# V

## Estevanico Sold into Slavery, His Conversion and His Coming to the New World

When Álvar Núñez Cabeza de Vaca and his three companions finally encounter Spaniards in Nueva Galicia, in Northwestern Mexico, in 1536, after nearly a decade of life among indigenous tribes in North America that began with the collapse of the Panilo de Narváez expedition to Florida. Cabeza de Vaca is careful to characterize their entire experience as one of perilous imprisonment.

—Richard A. Gordon, "Following Estevanico"

The Black-skinned Moor, Estevanico, may have been purchased from slave raiders who worked the African Coast. Or he may have been taken captive in one of the frequent military clashes between Spain and Morocco that continued long after the Moors were expelled from the Iberian Peninsula in 1492.

When Estevanico was purchased or captured, it was by the Portuguese and must have been sometime after 1513 when Portugal took control of Morocco, particularly Azemmour, his hometown. By 1522, Estevanico was living with Señor Dorantes, and five years later, he accompanied the Don to the New World.

We also know that Estevanico, or "Little Stephen," also called "The Black," was a Moroccan slave who accompanied de Vaca on his odyssey through the American southwest. Their visit to the Seven Cities of Gold preceded the exploration of Coronado in 1540.

There is very little available information about the early life of Estevanico and his being sold into slavery by the Portuguese to the Spanish. Prior to 1527, it is likely that he was baptized in Spain and given the name Little Stephen. These facts must have transpired sometime between 1513, when the Portuguese gained control of Azemmour, and 1521 or 1522 when the Moroccan was sold to the Spanish as a slave by nobleman Andrés Dorantes de Carranza.

Another fact that is certain is that he became the slave of de Carranza and that Estevanico accompanied his master as a member of an expedition to the New World organized by Pánfilo de Narváez.[108]

The article "Estebanico Zemmouri: The First Moroccan to Reach the American Soil" by Latifa Babas suggested that in 1527 "Mustapha was given a new name."[109] She made that claim, however, without including any source that proves the claim. Other scholars say the name change must have come much earlier, closer to the Portuguese control of Azemmour or the slave's original sale to Señor Dorantes.

What we do know about the period around the birth of Estevanico is that the Arabs of Morocco of whom the slave's family were members, were in constant warfare with their Spanish and Portuguese neighbors to the north. Sometime around 1513, Estevanico was captured by the Portuguese and sold into slavery to the Spanish, probably in Spain.

Estevanico was regularly referred to as "The Black," so it may well be that some of his ancestors were sub-Saharan since there were many years of contact between the Arabs and Berbers of North Africa and the Black people who lived south of the Sahara Desert.

The primary source regarding Narváez's expedition to the New World is the 1542 *Relación*, the first-person account of Cabeza de Vaca, who was the expedition's treasurer. De Vaca had written the report hoping to secure a royal commission in the New World for his labors. In fact, he subsequently received a royal commission to be the governor of the territories along the Rio de la Plata in South America.

The Rio de la Plata is a muddy estuary on the Parana and Uruguay Rivers and forms part of the border between Argentina and Uruguay. The rich estuary supports both capital cities of Buenos Aires and Montevideo.

In 1555, de Vaca published a revised edition of the *Relación*, often referred to as *Los Naufragios*, or "The Ship-wrecked Ones."[110] He created this document to support his defense against legal charges brought against him by companions on his expedition to the Rio de la Plata.[111]

A third primary source of the expedition of Narváez to the New World is a narrative written by Gonzalo Fernández de Oviedo y Valdés, who is usually referred to as "Oviedo." He participated in the colonization of the Caribbean as the official historiographer of Spain. Oviedo supplied his own version of what was called the "Joint Report" of explorations of Spain in the New World. Oviedo published his version in Book thirty-five, chapters one to six of what was called *Historia General y Natural de las Indias*.[112]

With the identification of these three primary sources, we can return to our explication of the first voyage of Pánfilo de Narváez to the New World in 1527 and 1528.

Narváez's first expedition consisted of approximately three hundred sailors. They left Spain on June 17, 1527, in five "caravela," medium-sized ships with a low draft and angular sails. The caravela was very fast and only required a small crew to keep it afloat. Both the Spanish and Portuguese models of the caravela were based on a mid-fifteenth-century fishing boat designed by Prince Henry the Navigator of Portugal, also known as Infante Dom Henrique (1394–1460).

In mid-April 1528, the Narváez expedition landed near present-day Tampa Bay, Florida. Narváez was permanently separated from his support vessels, and he and his men marched up the inner Florida coast. By late summer, they arrived at the mouth of the Wakulla River in the Florida panhandle.

Meanwhile, the surviving crew of the other Narváez vessels numbered about two hundred and fifty men, the others having died or were killed by the native people. The conditions of the survivors were so bad that Narváez chose to slaughter his horses for food. Because of the damage to his ships in the passage, Narváez and his men built five makeshift rafts, or barges, with the intention of sailing along the Gulf coast toward Mexico. The five rafts left Florida on the morning of September 22, 1528, and the craft containing Estevanico—what was called Boat Number Three—was placed under the joint command of Dorantes and Alonso del Castillo Maldonado.[113]

After a month at sea, Boat Number Three landed on Galveston Island off the coast of present-day Texas. By the spring of 1529, those three men, Estevanico, Durante and Maldonado, were the only three survivors. They traveled by foot down the Texas coast to Matagorda Bay.[114]

The three Spanish sailors were later captured by Indians and turned into slaves. The captors were members of the Coahuiltecan Tribe, known for being great warriors. Later, the Spanish sailors escaped their captors and fled south on foot and alone to what is now the Falcon Lake Reservoir.[115] The reservoir is now a 575-acre state park located north of Roma, Texas, an area of steep sandstone bluffs above the north banks of the Rio Grande.[116] The escape from the Native Americans happened on September 15, 1534, while their captors were busy harvesting prickly pears.[117] They made their escape and were taken in by another tribe who had heard of the abilities of the three in medical matters and healing. Cabeza de Vaca reported these abilities:

> Our fame spread throughout the area, and all the Indians who heard about it came looking for us so we could heal them and bless their children.... People came from many places, and they told us that we were truly "Children of the Sun."[118]

To this point, Dorantes and Estevanico had not participated in the healings. But they soon joined in when the Native Americans made requests. It appears as though some of the healings involved the utilization of minor early sixteenth-century surgical techniques. On one occasion, they opened a man's heart to remove an arrowhead. De Vaca tells us:

> The entire village came to see the arrowhead, and they sent it further inland so other people could see the miracle.[119]

De Vaca added this in his narrative:

> Because of this cure, they made many dances and religious festivals as is their custom... And this gave us a certain standing throughout the land that they esteemed and valued us to their utmost capacity.[120]

The Spaniards thought it was wise to make Estevanico the conduit or "middleman" between them and the Native Americans. This was principally because of the Black man's facility to learn languages. In fact, by the time of their escape from slavery, the Moroccan slave had mastered six Indian dialects, in addition to his abilities in his native Arabic, Portuguese and Spanish.

Again, Cabeza de Vaca explained the Spaniards' communication with the Native Americans, as opposed to that of the Moroccan slave, Estevanico. De Vaca commented:

> We enjoyed a great deal of authority and dignity among the Indians, and to maintain this, we spoke very little to them. The Black man always spoke to them, ascertaining which way to go and all the other things we wanted to know.[121]

As the medical miracles multiplied, so did the gifts the group received from the Indians. The four were held in such awe that they could lay claim to anything they saw in their travels. One of the most important gifts they received was from a medicine man in the Arbadaos Tribe, a people who made their home on the banks of the Rancho River near present-day Big Springs, Texas.[122]

The medicine man presented Estevanico with a sacred gourd filled with stones and an engraved copper rattle. These objects greatly added to his abilities as a shaman. Cabeza de Vaca tells us this:

> From this point on, the Black man carried his gourd and rattle with him. The Indians said those objects have powers that came from the Heavens.[123]

In his *Relación*, Cabeza de Vaca also makes some interesting comments about the Arbadaos Tribe. For example, he says they have no inkling of time "either by the Sun or the Moon."[124] The three Europeans and one African lived with the Arbadaos for eight months. But at the end of the eight months when the prickly pears had ripened in mid-June of 1535, Estevanico and Cabeza de Vaca escaped. A short time later, Castillo and Dorantes joined them.

Eventually, the four men traveled west into present-day Mexico and Texas. These four men were the first Europeans and the first

Black man to enter the American West. They had walked nearly two thousand miles since their landing in Florida until they finally came to a Spanish settlement named "Sinaloa," a state in the northwest region of Mexico.[125]

From there, the Spanish explorers traveled one thousand miles to Mexico City, farther inland. The group met up with another party of Spaniards in March of 1536 before they entered Mexico City on July 24, 1536. The four explorers were well-received by the Viceroy of Mexico, Antonio Mendoza, who was intrigued by the group's stories of the wealthy cities to the north. Cabeza de Vaca returned to Spain while Castillo and Dorantes married and settled down in Mexico.[126]

At that time, Dorantes either sold or gave Estevanico to the Viceroy Mendoza. Mendoza had decided to send an expedition north to the fabled Seven Cities of Gold. A Franciscan friar named Fray Marcos de Niza was chosen to lead the expedition north to what would become the United States.[127] It is likely that Estevanico was freed at the same time becoming the first freed slave in America, most likely by Señor Dorantes.

Fray de Niza appointed Estevanico to be his scout and guide. In the fall of 1538, they went north to the town of Culiacán, where the king of Spain had recently appointed Francisco Vazquez de Coronado governor. When Estevanico left for Cibola, he was accompanied by several Sinaloan Indians who had a particular task to fulfill, as we shall see in the next section of this study. Sinaloa was the name of the northwest Mexican state where New Spain was situated. Many of the native Indians that accompanied Estevanico, most likely, were Sinaloan Indians.

Estevanico and Fray Marcos left Culiacán on the morning of March 7, 1539. The Moroccan slave was sent ahead on a scouting mission to scout the trail. Four days later, Native American runners, part of Estevanico's party, returned to Fray Marcos to inform him that he had heard that he was only a "thirty days march from Cibola," the first of the Cities of Gold. Estevanico asked the Franciscan to join him on the march.[128]

In conclusion, then, Estevanico of Azemmour spoke three languages fluently—Arabic, Portuguese and Spanish—and during his travels in North America from 1528 until 1539, it is likely he acquired a working knowledge of at least another six Native American languages. Among these languages were those spoken by the Coahuiltecan Tribe, the tongue of the Avavares People, as well as the language of the Mariame Tribe, which shared many words with the Avavares.

Additionally, it is also probably the case that Estevanico acquired the use of the Karankawa people's language, as well as some of the Sonoran Indian languages, of which there are seven. Knowing one of these groups would be similar to learning Arabic if one knew Syriac or Aramaic.

The seven languages of the Sonoran Desert include Mayo, Cucapa, Papago, Seri, Yaqui, Pima and Guarijio. If Estevanico learned any of these seven in one Sonora village, he would have had some fluency in the next village as well, or even, perhaps, one far away in the same desert, for they arose from the same sources.

This brings us to Chapter Six of this study, in which we will give a more detailed account than the one we have earlier provided in the Introductory Essay of the life and death of Estevanico, the first Black man in America.

# VI
## The Death of Estevanico

Estevanico's legacy is nothing if not ambiguous. So was his
personal experience. He was a Black African slave—
Christianized but Arabic speaking—who helped Álvar Núñez
Cabeza de Vaca and two other Castilians of the ill-fated 1527
Pánfilo de Narváez expedition.

—Rolena Adorno, "Estevanico's Legacy"

There are many things about the death of Estevanico about which we
can be sure. There are also several other questions about the end of
the Moroccan slave's life, about which we are less certain. Among the
things we are certain of is when Estevanico died, which appears to be
in late March 1539. We can also be certain where he died, and that is in
a village called Cibola, or Hawikuh, which the Zuni Indians controlled
at that time.

We also can be sure that Fray Marcos de Niza and Estevanico left
Mexico City to travel north to Arizona and New Mexico in the service
of Antonio de Mendoza, Viceroy of Mexico. He sent the pair, along
with some Indian companions, to explore the Seven Cities of Gold. As
indicated earlier, Fray de Niza was in charge of the expedition.[129]

We also know that on March 7, 1539, de Niza sent Estevanico
ahead on the trail to scout out and guide the friar and his men to come
later. It appears that the Black man had strict orders not to enter Cibola
without his Franciscan leader. But despite these strict instructions, the
Moroccan pressed ahead to the village of Cibola, or Hawikuh, about

twenty kilometers or twelve miles southwest of what today is called the "Zuni Pueblo."[130]

In the account provided by Cabeza de Vaca, he adds several other facts about the events leading up to the homicide of Estevanico. De Vaca tells us that de Niza told the slave not to venture "more than one hundred and fifty miles from the base camp."[131] Secondly, de Niza sent Estevanico "to see whether information can be acquired about what we were seeking," meaning, of course, gold and silver.

Thirdly, if the slave learned of "some inhabitants with riches, he should stay put and send back word. Finally, after receiving word from a messenger that Estevanico had found Cibola, Fray Marcos chased his disobedient subordinate, only to learn a few days later that the slave from Morocco, Estevanico, was dead.[132]

The *Ashiwi* people, or what today are called the Zuni Tribe, live in the Zuni Pueblo located on the Zuni River, a tributary of the Colorado River in western New Mexico. The Zuni Pueblo is about thirty-five miles south of Gallup, New Mexico, and currently has a population of about twelve thousand people, with 80 percent of them being Zuni Native Americans.[133]

Today, the poverty line, as defined by the US Government, 43 percent of the Zuni Pueblo population live below that line. The Zuni remain famous for their art, particularly their pottery and jewelry. They also continue to practice many of the traditional Zuni religious traditions, like ceremonies and dances that are now performed for tourists.

The Hawikuh Pueblo was the first village seen by the Spanish explorers and, in particular, by Estevanico. It was believed to be one of the legendary villages of gold sought by Antonio de Mendoza, Fray de Niza and, of course, Estevanico, who was the first non-Native human to reach this pueblo.

The people of Hawikuh spoke a dialect of the Zuni language, also called *Shiwi*. The dialect is still spoken by about ten thousand people, mostly in New Mexico and much smaller numbers in parts of eastern Arizona.[134]

For four hundred years, going back to the time that Estevanico went to Hawikuh and beyond that time, the Zuni people have lived by agriculture. They have a cycle of religious ceremonies that take precedence over everything else. Their religious beliefs are mostly centered on three main gods—the Earth-Mother, the Sun-Father and the Moon Light-Giving Mother. The Sun is especially worshipped. In fact, the Zuni word for "light" and "sun" are the same word.[135]

The main rituals in Zuni culture are related to four "Rites of Passage." These are birth, the coming of age, marriage and death. Every four years, the Zuni also make what is known as the "Barefoot Religious Walk" to what is called *Kolhu*, or *Walawa*, Zuni Heaven.[136] A detached portion of the 12,500-acre Zuni Reservation is reserved for the practice of these rituals. A four-day ritual is celebrated at the time of the summer solstice.[137]

Another barefoot pilgrimage conducted annually for centuries by the Zuni people and other southwestern Indian peoples is known as the "Barefoot Walk to the Salt Lake." It is a ritual that celebrates the harvesting of salt during the dry months and for other religious purposes. The lake is home to the Salt Mother, or what the Zunis call *Ma'l Oyattsik'i*. Many ancient pueblo roads and trails ended at the Great Salt Lake.

All of these ceremonies and rituals were part of the belief system of the people living at Cibola/Hawikuh when Estevanico entered the pueblo in late March of 1539. Another thing about which we can be certain is that the Moroccan hero of this Study was murdered by Zuni warriors in the pueblo.

What is left unknown is why the Zuni chief ordered that Estevanico be killed. Another mystery about the death of Estevanico is why his Franciscan boss, Fray de Niza—when he heard of the death of the Black man—immediately decided to return to Mexico City rather than traveling ahead to the Seven Cities of Gold as had been their plan.

In his *Relación*, de Vaca tells the following facts about the death of Estevanico that he had heard from two Indians reporting back to the Franciscan. Firstly, before his arrival, Estevanico, with his gourd and rattle in hand, fully expected the Zuni Indians to worship him as the other tribes had done.[138]

Secondly, the Zuni chief reacted with scorn, and some reports say he threw the gourd and rattle to the ground and, in the process, broke them. Thirdly, it appears that Estevanico could understand enough of the Zuni dialect to realize that he and his entourage would not be allowed into the pueblo. Fourthly, the chief ordered that they be taken to a small hut on the edge of the village.[139]

Fifthly, for three days, they were denied food and water while the council of elders decided what to do with them. They finally agreed that members of Estevanico's entourage would all be let go, but the strange Black man should be murdered.

Finally, on the fourth day, a team of bowmen was sent to the hut where the Moroccan was held captive, and he was struck by several arrows. According to a man named Alarcon, the Spaniard who interviewed one of the two Indians who reported the death to Fray de Niza, said:

> The village chief appropriated all of the Moroccan's belongings. These included four green dishes, together with two dogs, and several pieces of turquois and pearls, as well as other things of the Black man.

Five hundred years later, a centenarian Zuni oral historian told the following story in a television documentary called *Surviving Columbus: The Story of Pueblo People*:

> The people who lived at the steaming springs had a giant who led them, who walked ahead of them as their guide. And the people from Hahihipinnkiya had twin war gods as their leaders. The Sun Father knew that the giant could not be killed, so that when they brought their weapons to the twin war gods they pierced them with arrows, but the giant would not die.... Then the Sun Father said, "His heart is in the Gourd rattle. The Gourd is in his heart, and if you destroy it you will destroy him, and your way will be clear." Then, the young warrior stepped forward from the fighting and shot the Gourd rattle. And the giant fell and all the people ran away.[140]

One only wonders, of course, if this is actually a first-person account of the murder of Estevanico of Morocco. The Black man was the giant, and the Zuni chief played the Sun Father.

Although we do not know for sure that this narrative is about Estevanico, we can be certain that four hundred and fifty years after the Moroccan's death at the pueblo of Hawikuh, his image returned to the great Southwest in the form of a piece of clay sculpture by artist John Houser.[141] After plaster impressions, waxing and testing, a bronze replica of Estevanico, the first Black man in America, was finally cast. It is currently housed at the XII Travelers Gallery in El Paso, Texas. The large Texas African-American History Memorial was erected in 2016 at the intersection of West 11th Street and Congress Avenue in Austin, Texas. The piece of art by Mr. Houser is on the grounds of the Texas State Capital in Austin.[142] We will say more about John Houser and his art in a later section of this study.

Three other questions remain about the death of Estevanico. First, why did the Zuni Indians murder the Moroccan? Secondly, why did the Franciscan de Niza not continue on to visit Cibola after he heard of the tragic death of the man he called "Black Stephen?" It appears that after he heard the news, de Niza immediately returned to Mexico City and, a short time later, to Spain.

Thirdly, why did the Franciscan agree to accompany Coronado in the latter's exploration of the Seven Cities of Gold the following year in 1540? We will discuss each of these three questions in the order we have given them here.

In 1539 and immediately afterward, there were several theories about why the council of Zuni elders chose to have Estevanico killed. Among those theories are the following:

1. Estevanico told the Zuni that a large army with great weapons followed him.
2. The Zuni Chief did not believe in the efficacy of the slave's healing powers.
3. The Zuni council of elders in Cibola wanted the possessions of Estevanico.
4. The Zuni believed that Estevanico was a spy from another tribe that was an enemy of the Zuni.
5. The Zuni council and chief were skeptical that the White European Spanish would send a Black man to represent them.

6.  Estevanico's blackness and his healing powers were seen as elements of black magic and the occult.
7.  Estevanico had too much of a fondness for the many Native-American women and girls he encountered.
8.  Estevanico demanded bribes from the Zuni.
9.  The Zuni elders and chief were motivated principally by fear.

We will comment on each of these nine theories and why they may be plausible, beginning with the claim that Estevanico was said to be a scout for a large army with great weapons that were to follow him. In one sense, theory number 1 was true in that Estevanico was to be followed by Friar de Niza and his entourage. They were to follow the Moroccan to the first of the Seven Cities of Gold at Cibola. But the contingent of de Niza could hardly be called a "large army with great weapons." But if the chief and elders believed that claim, that may have been reason enough for murdering Estevanico.

That theory number 2 was true is supported by the claim that the Zuni chief is said to have thrown the healing gourd and rattle to the ground so that they would be smashed. There are many possible reasons why the chief would have done such a thing, but we cannot further speculate at this point in the discussion of the matter.

Theory number 3 appears to have been true because when Francisco Coronado went to Cibola in 1540, all of Estevanico's possessions were in the hands of the chief. These included, among other things, pieces of turquois, a set of green dinner plates, a metal bell, and the Moroccan's two Greyhound dogs. So maybe they killed him for his money.[143]

Francisco Vazquez de Coronado, Conquistador.
Courtesy of Look and Learn / Bridgeman Images.

Theory number 4 is certainly a plausible one. In the pueblo life of the Southwest, it was very easy to acquire enemies, and certainly, the Black man could have been a spy for one of those enemies. It is also easy to comprehend that the Zuni elders might have been skeptical that the White Europeans would send a Black man to represent them. Beyond that, however, little else can be said.

Theory number 6, the pre-literate nature of the early modern Zuni people could very well have come into play regarding the killing of Estevanico. There are reports that the Zuni made a Black *kachina*, or doll, to represent the body of Estevanico. For the Zuni, to destroy the doll was to destroy the Black man, along with the many associations of blackness among the people of the Zuni Pueblo.

There are also reports that the feathers associated with Estevanico's gourd and rattle were those of an owl, a bird associated with darkness and death in many pre-literate societies. Certainly, Sir James Frazer's "Law of Similarity" and "Law of Contagion" may have been at work in deciding why Estevanico was murdered on a morning in March 1539.

The fact that the Zuni elders are said to have ordered Estevanico's corpse be cut up into small pieces and distributed to the council members to be consumed by them—if true—would also be further evidence that the Zuni people were believers in Frazer's laws.

Regarding theory number 7, in several places in the *Relación*, de Vaca mentioned Estevanico's "fondness" of the Native women, as well as the slave's penchant for acquiring possessions and, in general, his lack of discipline. These aspects of Estevanico's life could not have made Marcos de Niza very happy, given the friar's dedication to the traditional Franciscan vows of poverty, chastity and obedience.[144]

One source even suggested that Estevanico had raped and then killed a Cochiti woman. But because of the Moroccan slave's reputation as a healer, the woman's family did not immediately pursue the matter. They told the Zuni chief that the Black man was an evil man who assaulted their women. So, the Zuni chief locked Estevanico in a hut on the edge of the pueblo while the elders debated over what they should do with him.

There are some sources that suggest that other Native American tribes were upset with Estevanico because he had molested, and even raped, some of the Indian females, and de Vaca mentions this as well in the narrative.[145]

Theory number 9 also appears to be a possible explanation as we tie it to theory number 8, that the Zunis—more than anything else— were afraid of Estevanico and the "army with great weapons" that may follow him. We also cannot discount the way that Estevanico presented himself. As Cabeza de Vaca tells us in his narrative, the Moroccan slave acquired a harem of native girls who followed in his wake. He adorned himself with "clusters of bright feathers and wore a crown of plumes on his head."[146]

Cabeza de Vaca added this about Estevanico's dress:

> Small bells were fashioned around his ankles that chimed as he walked, and coral and turquois ornaments presented to him by the Indians decorated his chest.[147]

Estevanico appears to have been a large Black man and must have made an impressive sight, particularly compared to the frugal garb and effects of the Franciscans. We also know that Estevanico participated in native ceremonies and festivals, and later the Zuni people instituted a ritual related to the coming to Cibola and his murder.

It is quite possible, of course, that some aspects of each of these nine theories may have been at work in regard to the demise of the Moroccan, Estevanico. It is also possible that none of them were at work. At this point in the scholarship of the matter, however, no definitive conclusions may be made about it.

One further point about the death of Estevanico is that one of the two men who reported back to Marcos de Niza that the slave was dead was the Moroccan's closest friend on the mission, a man named García López de Cárdenas who also gave testimony that was recorded in 1546 about the murder. The testimony was taken during a trial of Cárdenas, who was charged with treating the Native Americans with cruelty during the de Niza mission. He was convicted, served a thirty-month sentence and paid a fine of eight hundred gold ducats. The money was to be used to finance religious and charitable activities.[148]

One final point that must be raised regarding Cabeza de Vaca's testimony, as well as that of Friar Marcos de Niza, is how reliable they should be considered. Historian Pedro de Castañeda found little about de Niza's account that could be considered reliable.[149] A year later, in 1540, in a letter to Viceroy Mendoza, Francisco Coronado observed, "I can assure you that he has not told the truth in a single thing he has said."[150] In fact, even explorer Hernán Cortés, at least according to scholars Adorno and Pautz, called the friar a "liar."[151]

In his biography of the first Black man in America called *Estevanico, The Black*, John Upton Terrell observed that:

> Some documents state that Fray Marcos had become ill and thought it best to return to Mexico City for treatment.[152]

Pedro de Castañeda, however, bluntly declared that the celebrated Franciscan went back "because he did not think it was safe for him to stay near Cibola."[153] There is probably no further supposition to be made about the matter than this.

When Coronado and his entourage got to Cibola after having been in the pueblo for six weeks, the explorer wrote a letter to Mendoza saying, "The seven cities are actually seven little villages. They are all within a radius of five leagues." About the people of the Hawikuh Pueblo, Coronado wrote, "They are fairly large and quite intelligent."[154] Francisco Coronado concluded his letter to the Spanish viceroy of Mexico:

> As far as I can judge, it does not appear to me that there is any hope of getting gold or silver, but I trust in God that, if there is any, we shall get our share of it.[155]

In another place in the same essay, Mr. Logan concluded:

> The preponderance of evidence would seem to warrant the conclusion that fear of Estevanico and those who had sent him forward was the principal reason that led the Indians to kill him.[156]

As the weeks passed on Coronado's expedition, he learned of pueblos farther east, many of them located on the river that would later be called the *Rio Grande*, or the "Great River." As August 1540 drew to a close, he welcomed two visitors to his camp. The first was a striking young chief he would call *Bigotes*, or "Whiskers."[157]

The other visitor to the Coronado camp was an old tribal chief that the Spanish explorer named *Cacique*, or the "Boss." Coronado learned that the pair came from a place called *Cicuyw*, now known as *Pecos*. It was a large and important pueblo and trading center, again to the east, beyond the Rio Grande.[158]

Coronado Seeking the Seven Cities of Gold. Painting courtesy of Jim Carson, www.jimcarsonstudio.com.

Francisco Coronado's expedition was important for our purpose at hand chiefly because what he says he had discovered has been, more or less, contradicted by what Fray Marcos de Niza related about the Seven Cities of Gold. One way to see that is that Estevanico was instructed to communicate his findings by sending back crosses to de Niza's party to indicate the booty found on the slave's travels.[159]

One day a cross arrived that was as tall as a man. All the other previous crosses had been much smaller. This caused Fray de Niza to step up his pace so he could join his scout, Estevanico. But a year later, with the explorations of Coronado, it was discovered that Estevanico's employment of the large cross was a fraud.

One Zuni legend still told in the Zuni Pueblo is that when Estevanico arrived at Cibola, he mistook the corn that was drying on the pueblo's roofs for gold and thus sent the larger cross back to Cabeza de Vaca. There may have been other reasons for the large cross, but that is the Zuni answer that is still extant.

The theory that there are seven cities of gold in North America is a very old idea first proposed by North African Arab geographer and cartographer Muhammad al-Idrisi (ca. 1100–1165). In his celebrated *Tabula Rogeriana*, he claimed one of the first world maps in Africa and Europe. Thus, the idea of cities of gold had existed in North Africa and Iberia for at least five hundred years before Estevanico's arrival in Cibola.

The eighth theory listed above regarding why Estevanico was murdered, stating that it occurred out of fear, was suggested by Rayford W. Logan in the journal *Phylon* in an essay entitled "Estevanico: Negro Discoverer of the Southwest. A Reappraisal." At the close of his essay, Logan wrote:

> Estevanico was a Negro in the North American sense of the word. He was as hardy as any of the Spaniards. He became a skilled medicine man and was killed because the Zuni elders feared him.[160]

One final opinion about the death of Estevanico comes from a scholar named Juan Francisco Maura, who, in a book written about the de Niza expedition to Cibola, suggested that the Zunis did not kill Estevanico. Instead, they helped him gain his freedom.[161] This may be a plausible view if the Moroccan slave had not already gained his independence three years earlier in 1536, at least according to some Spanish documents that are extant.

At any rate, there is no information about where Estevanico is buried. Even the village of Hawikuh no longer exists, for it was abandoned in 1670 after the series of wars that the Zunis fought with the Spanish, beginning with Coronado in the spring and summer of 1540 and then Pedro de Castañeda and others.

Given the fact that Estevanico's body was reportedly cut up into small pieces to be consumed by the Zuni elders, there may not have been a burial of Estevanico beyond this dismemberment and evisceration.

This brings us to Chapter Seven of this study on the life of Estevanico, the first Black man in America, in which we will say more about the Moroccan's role as an interpreter and a translator in the great Southwest of what would become the United States of America.

# VII
# Estevanico as Translator and Interpreter

In this regard, the figure of Estevanico himself became emblematic
as he was portrayed by Cabeza de Vaca and whether the "gentle-
man from Jerez de la Frontera," intended it or not. Estevanico is
characterized in this narrative for acting and surviving with his wits.

—Rolena Adorno, "Estevanico's Legacy"

The earliest Spanish translators in the New World were captured natives.
One fine example of this phenomenon can be seen on Columbus' fourth
voyage in 1502, where the Spaniards seized a native man named Yumbe,
who then served as a guide for as long as they were in territories whose
languages Yumbe could understand. He provided the Spaniards with
valuable knowledge of the places and cultures that were in Yumbe's
purview.

When Yumbe became unable to communicate with the local
population, the Spanish allowed him to return home. Some sources
refer to Yumbe as a *cacique*, or "boss," "who seemed to be the wisest
man among them and of the greatest authority."[162]

In the Introductory Essay earlier in this study, we indicated that
many people in the historical record spoke of the Moroccan's facility
for languages. This is not surprising given the fact that after his
capture by the Portuguese and his selling to the Spanish, he apparently
was able to accommodate himself into Portuguese and Spanish very
quickly.

There is now growing scholarly evidence that people who know
many languages have a better facility for learning new tongues,

particularly if they are in the same language family. Thus, for example, if a person knows Classical Hebrew, then Aramaic, Syriac and Arabic become much easier to learn because they all rely on the same tri-consonantal roots.

Thus, for example, the Semitic root SLM is the source of words related to "peace." The Classical Hebrew *Shalom* and the Arabic *Salaam* come from this same root.[163] Similarly, it may well have been the case that Estevanico was able to learn many American Indian dialects because he already had a great facility for tongues other than his natural one.

In his *Relación*, Cabeza de Vaca wrote several times about the Moroccan's facility for languages. At one point, he mentions that Estevanico was able to acquire "at least six of the Indian languages."[164]

The first of these may have been the tongue of those who enslaved the survivors of the Narváez expedition—the Coahuiltecan, who lived southwest of the Guadalupe River. If the Moroccan lived with the Coahuiltecan for an extended time, as all four survivors did, it would not have taken long to acquire their tongue.[165] The Cochiti Tribe and its pueblo is on the west bank of the Rio Grande, about thirty miles west of Santa Fe, New Mexico. The population of the Cochiti Pueblo is about three hundred. The tribe occupies a land grant from the government that includes more than twenty-four thousand acres of land. This land was originally ceded to the Cochiti People by Spain, but it was confirmed in 1864 by the United States Government. Given the long period that Estevanico spent with the Cochiti, he, most assuredly, developed a fluency in their language.

The Cochiti language is one of a group of seven pueblo dialects that are sometimes divided into "Eastern *Keres*" that include the dialects in the Cochiti, San Felipe pueblos, as well as the Kewa, Zia, and Santa Ana pueblos. Today there are about thirteen thousand Keres speakers in these pueblos. "Western *Keres*," on the other hand, includes the pueblos of Acomo and Laguna, where approximately five thousand people speak these two dialects that are known as *Aak'u* and *Kawaika*.

These seven dialects of the *Keres* language are members of the same language family. If one knows one or two of these dialects, the other five or six become much easier to learn, much like Estevanico's transition from Portuguese to Castilian Spanish in the early 1520s.

Similarly, there is sufficient evidence that Estevanico learned a dialect of the Zuni languages so he could communicate with his captors. Unlike most Native-American languages, the speakers of *Shiwi'ma*, the native name of Zuni, is still spoken by a significant number of children today, so it is less threatened with endangerment than other Native tongues. Nevertheless, there are several dialects of *Shiwi*, and Estevanico must have understood some of them.

The Moroccan interpreter and translator was also able to speak directly to members of the Avavares Tribe, the Plains Indians he lived with for a while before he went to Cibola.[166] We do know that the Avavares were one of the first Native Americans to be appreciative with Estevanico's healing abilities.

It was among the Avavares Indians that Estevanico spent his final seven months in Texas, at least according to his biographers. The Avavares, however, spoke a very different language and may have been at odds with other Indians like the Mariames, for example. The Mariame enjoyed the harvesting and fishing of tuna, particularly on the southernmost bend of the Nueces River, only a few day's walk from the Rio Grande.

Cabeza de Vaca wrote of living among the Mariames. He observed:

The land is so rough and overgrown that many times we would gather in the brush forests morsels and when we were finished with that, we often gathered wood. It was so difficult, however, that after a while, I could not take it out, neither on my back nor by dragging it.[167]

About the Avavares and the explorers' that stayed with them, de Vaca told us:

Among them, we were always well treated, although we had to dig up whatever we would eat, and we carried our own loads of water and wood. Their dwellings and food supplies are much like those of the previous ones, though they do go about hungrier.[168]

Cabeza de Vaca does, however, point out one difference that is distinct for the Mariames people,

> Like them, we went around naked and at night we covered our-
> selves with deer skins. Of the eight months we were with them,
> we suffered great hunger in six of them.

De Vaca goes on to describe another Native American tribe that he called the *Maliacones*. He described them as a people who,

> ...suffered much hunger, and not less, but even greater than
> during the previous seven years. The cause of these Indians' pre-
> dicament was that they were not near water, where they could
> kill fish and thus, they did not eat anything but roots.[169]

De Vaca also concluded this about the Maliacones:

> These Indians have a greater trouble of keeping alive than any
> of the others who mostly eat fish. And there the boys are so thin
> and swollen that they resemble toads. But at least among these
> Indians those Christians were well treated and they permitted
> them to live in freedom and to do everything that they wanted.[170]

The Maliacones, whose name in Spanish means "Evil Ones," is only mentioned in the narrative of Alvar Nunez Cabeza de Vaca. The precise location of this tribe is not known, but the available evidence suggests an area near the lower Nueces River. Another problem in identifying the Maliacones is that their existence is not referred to anywhere, but clearly, the tribe was not seen in a positive light by Señor Cabeza de Vaca.

Estevanico also became fluent in the language of the Karankawa, at least according to his biographers. The Karankawa were made up of five separate tribes and dialects related by language and culture. These were called the *Caranecaguases*, the Karankawa proper, the *Cucos*, the *Cujanes*, the *Guapites*, and the *Copanes*.[171]

In Estevanico's time, these five tribes depended on fishing and hunting. They particularly consumed the fish and shellfish found in the shallow bays and lagoons of the central Texas coast. The dugout canoes of the Karankawa were not designed for travel in the open Gulf of

Mexico. We do know that the Karankawa Tribes lived in wigwams, circular structures with pole frames covered with mats or hides.

It is likely that Estevanico quickly learned one or more of the Karankawa dialects. Two other aspects of these five tribes are significant. First, unlike many of the other Native American people described in this study, the Karankawa did not have a complex political structure. And secondly, the warriors of these five tribes were particularly tall. In fact, many of these men were six feet or taller and were also noted for their great strength.[172]

The Franciscan friar Marcos de Niza also wrote about the Indians of *Chichilticalli*, with whom Estebanico, the friar, and their entourage stayed for a time. Again, of course, it is quite likely that it would not have taken long for the Moroccan to develop a facility in the tongue of the Chichilticalli.[173]

One of the first groups of Indians that the Spaniards' party first encountered was the Apalachee of northwest Florida. Cabeza de Vaca points out that with this group, Estevanico was already honing his skills in Indian sign language that would become very important with Native Americans he would meet later in Arizona and New Mexico.

Finally, three other groups of Native American tribes also can claim some contact with Estevanico of Morocco, the first Black man in America. These are the Mariame Tribe near San Antonio Bay in Texas, the Sonoran Indians, who lived in the Sonoran Desert of Mexico, and the Arbadaos Tribe, near Big Springs, Texas, who gave Estevanico the sacred gourd and magical rattle that he carried into many Indian villages.

If any or all of these conclusions are true, then in addition to his native Arabic and Portuguese and Spanish, Estevanico was also able to acquire a facility of at least seven or eight Native American tongues and perhaps as many as ten.

In addition to these spoken languages, both de Vaca and Marcos de Niza also spoke of an ability that Estevanico acquired in his time with the various Native-American tribes through the use of sign language to communicate with the Native people. It is also said that he deployed implements of Native culture in order to communicate with—or even to impress—local tribes. So not all of Estevanico's communication skills were linguistic in nature.

Given what we have said earlier in the Introductory Essay in this study about Sir James Frazer and his "Law of Similarity" and "Law of Contagion," the work of Estevanico could best perhaps be seen as the junction of science, magic and religion, particularly in the reportedly healing activities of Estevanico's party during his travels.

One final point about Estevanico as a translator and interpreter was made in an article by Gabriel Gonzales Núñez in which he wrote,

> What we generally understand to be an interpreter's role today does not necessarily apply to that interpreters played in the fifteenth and sixteenth centuries, especially during the early stages of exploration and conquest in the Americas.[174]

Writer Núñez also points out:

> One must understand that our understanding of that role is, in all likelihood, fragmentary. This is so because information about interpreters is generally scarce in traditional historical sources, including sources that help to rebuild the history of the conquest of the Americas by Europeans.[175]

Mr. Núñez also points out that in facilitating from language to language, "Interpreters had little or no training."[176] Although this is true, by the time that Estevanico arrived in North America in 1528, he did have a kind of training in that from the time he became Señor Dorantes' slave in 1522 until the time he arrived in Florida six years later, he had to be able to communicate in first Portuguese and then Spanish with his captors.[177]

Now it is certainly true that learning a second language in the same language group, like Romance languages, in this case, is much easier than starting from scratch. And this most likely had something to do with the linguistic skills he acquired among the Native Americans. Learning the language or dialect of a group may turn out to be quite similar to the tongue spoken in the next city or pueblo. Estevanico surely must have understood this fact as he worked in communications with the Native Americans at the behest of the crown of Spain.

Let me tell a personal story to illustrate some of the points I am making. Many years ago, when I was a graduate student at Yale

University, I enrolled in a seminar course about the life and philosophy of Danish writer Soren Kierkegaard. The instructor of the course recommended—but did not require—that his students for this class also enroll in elementary Danish.

As far as I know, I was one of the few that conceded to the request. A few years later, I was in the Strand Bookstore in New York City, a place that has books from all over the world. So I went to where the Danish books were, and when I did so, I made a great discovery. Next to the Danish books, on either side were books in Swedish and Norwegian. And, lo and behold, I could read the titles and understand their content.

I might add that there were also Finish books in the same area of the store, in which I could not understand a word. It turns out, of course, that Danish, Swedish and Norwegian were in the same language group, while Finish was not a member of that group.

Similarly, I learned my first lessons in Classical Hebrew when I was in high school from the Semitic scholar William F. Albright. In graduate school, I continued to study Hebrew, as well as Aramaic and Syriac. These two languages were much easier to learn because the three tongues were in the same language group.

More than thirty years after the end of my university training, I set out in the 1990s to learn Classical Arabic, the language of Al-Qur'an. I found learning the language to be easier than I believed it would be. But it turns out that all Semitic languages—the language group to which all four of these tongues are members—Hebrew, Aramaic, Syriac and Arabic—are all members of the Semitic language group.

Now one way to understand this is when one discovers that every Semitic language is based on tri-consonantal roots, and they are the same roots in all four languages. Thus, the SLM root is the bases for words related to peace, like *Shalom* in Hebrew and *Salaam* in Arabic, for example.

We have told these personal stories because something like what I have related here must have been going on in the mind of Estevanico, in addition to what may have been a genetic ability to learn many tongues. In this sense, it is not at all surprising to me that the Moroccan slave, Estevanico, would turn out to have an uncanny ability to become adept in many Native American languages and dialects.

In conclusion, then, Estevanico of Azemmour spoke three languages fluently, Arabic, Portuguese and Spanish, and in the course of his travels in North America from 1528 until 1539, it is likely that he acquired a working knowledge of at least another six Native American tongues. Among these languages were those spoken by the Coahuiltecan Tribe, the tongue of the Avavares, as well as the language of the Mariame Tribe, which shared many words with the Avavares.

Additionally, it is probably also the case that Estevanico acquired the use of the Karankawa people's language, as well as some of the Sonoran Indian languages, of which there are seven. To know one of these groups would be similar to learning Arabic if one already knows Syriac or Aramaic.

The seven languages of the Sonoran Desert include Mayo, Cucapa, Papago, Seri, Yaqui, Pima and Guarijio. If Estevanico learned any of these seven in one Sonoran village, he would have had some fluency in the next village as well, or even perhaps, one far away in the same desert for those who arose from the same historical sources.

Some of the Native languages of southern Texas and northern Mexico are what scholars call "isolates." These are languages that are so individual and peculiar that they appear to have been "isolated" from other areas and thus developed independently. Two of the largest and most important of these are the tongues spoken by the Coahuiltecan and the Karankawa.

The Zuni language—the tongue of those who captured and murdered Estevanico—at least according to some scholars—is also among the isolate languages of the American Southwest Native Americans. The indigenous name of the Zuni people and language is *Shiwi*. It was spoken mostly in western New Mexico, where Estevanico was murdered by the Zuni, and eastern Arizona from the sixteenth to the nineteenth centuries.

Among the eight languages of the Sonoran Desert, one of those tongues is also an isolate. It is called Seri. It is thought to be the last surviving language of its linguistic family. The Seri language—its vocabulary and alphabet—was studied in the 1950s by Edward W. and Mary B. Moser, a linguist couple who worked for the Summer Institute of Linguistics, or SIL. Later, the work of the Mosers was revised by Stephen Marlett, who also worked for SLI.

Today, only two villages on the coast of the Sonoran Desert in Mexico speak the Seri language. Many unsuccessful attempts have been made to tie the Seri tongue to other Native-American languages, such as a theoretical "Hokan Language" family. But no concrete evidence has been found to connect Seri to other tongues. If Estevanico spoke and understood Seri alone, then he probably would not have been able to comprehend the other tongues in the same family in the Sonoran Desert. If he knew or understood any of the other seven Sonoran languages, then he would have had some facility in the other six, but not to the isolate Seri.

In summary, it appears that Estevanico, the Moroccan slave from Azemmour, had a profound knowledge of—or even mastery of—the following tongues: his native Arabic, Portuguese and Spanish, as well as the following Native-American languages and his likely level of each:

1. The Coahuiltecan tongue (moderate mastery)
2. The Zuni language (fluent)
3. The Avavares tongue (moderate mastery)
4. The Mariame language (fluent)
5. The Arbadaos tongue (fluent)
6. The Karankawa language (moderate mastery)
7. The Sonoran tongues (moderate mastery)

From this data, then, it appears that Estevanico was fluent in six different languages: Arabic, Portuguese, Spanish, Zuni, Mariame, and Arbadoas, and was moderately fluent in another four Native-American tongues, those of the Coahuiltecan, the Avavares, and the Karankawa peoples and some of the tongues of the Native-American Sonoran Desert, but we are not certain of which if any of these.

This brings us to Chapter Eight of this study of the Moroccan, Estevanico, the first Black man in America. In this chapter, we will make some observations about the influences and the historical significances of the life of Estevanico, or "Little Stephen," from the city of Azemmour, Morocco.

# VIII
# The Influences of the Life of Estevanico

The first White man that our people saw was a Black man.

—Joe S. Sando, *Pueblo Nations*

The many influences that Estevanico of Morocco had on subsequent American culture are many and wide. In this chapter, we will identify and discuss many of these influences and, at the end of this section, in Chapter Nine to follow, we will speak of the historical significance of the life, work and times of Estevanico.

It should be abundantly clear that the most important historical significance about the life of Estevanico is that he was the first Black man, as well as the first slave, in what would become the United States of America. Beyond those facts, however, the Moroccan's life also was instrumental in many other venues and ways of American life.

In this chapter, we will describe and discuss the influences he had on literature, music, art, sculpture, and in other endeavors. Earlier, for example, we spoke of the influence that Estevanico had on the sculptor John Houser who we will say more about later in this chapter.

In regard to literature, American writer Laila Lalami wrote and published a fictional account of the life of Estevanico of Azemmour in 2014.[178] In discussing her book, Ms. Lalami recently related,

There is little known about his background except for one line in Cabeza de Vaca's chronicle: "The fourth survivor is Estevanico, an Arab Negro from Azamor."[179]

One fact that supported the fictional attempt to tell the narrative of Estevanico is that Laila Lalami—like the Moroccan slave—is Moroccan American herself.

Ms. Lalami tells the story of Estevanico as a first-person narrative in the Moroccan slave's own words. She does a very good job speaking about the three distinct societies from which Estevanico came—African-Arab, European and Colonial America. But at the same time, she makes Estevanico the most moral of all the actors in her drama and the Spaniard the least moral.

In many ways, Ms. Lalami, in her *The Moor's Account*, appears to buy into the New Left philosophy of Oppressors and Oppressed, such as in "The 1619 Project" and Critical Race Theory. But she spends little space in her narrative of whether her chief character is to be numbered among the Oppressors or the Oppressed. The Native Americans in Ms. Lalami's account are homogeneous, and there are no subtle differences between tribes as there are in real life.

Nevertheless, she does give Estevanico an Arabic name, and she creates experiences that she envisioned the real, historical man must have encountered. But at the same time, Ms. Lalami is too preachy in places, such as his refusal to disavow his Native wife when many of her other characters have done so. Ultimately, she seems to be making a statement about Colonialism and Imperialism. She clearly wishes to correct the historical record that Native Americans are not to be seen as "Vicious Savages" and to replace it as "Noble Savages."

In one passage of her narrative, Estevanico is contemplating the way of life among the Spaniards. She tells us through the Moroccan slave:

> How strange, I remember thinking how utterly strange were the ways of the Castilians—just by saying that something is so, they believed that it was. I know now that these conquerors, like many others before them, and no doubt like others after, gave speeches not to voice the truth but to create it.[180]

Again, Ms. Lalami appears to be condemning the Spaniards' way of life while at the same time holding to the New Left doctrine that "There is no objective truth, only points of view." This principle is another of the foundational ideas of Critical Race Theory and "The 1619 Project," along with the idea that race is the most fundamental aspect of identity and that the binary of Oppressors and Oppressed are at the heart of most conflict.[181]

A second literary source comes from poet Jeffrey Yang, who published a poem entitled "Estevanico." The Spanish explorer Álvar Núñez Cabeza de Vaca narrates the poem. It consists of fifty-two free-verse lines that recount the narrative of his years of exploration in the New World, including the Moroccan's roles as a healer and a scout or guide.[182]

The first modern American biography of Estevanico was written and completed in 1968 by John Upton Terrell. It was called *Estevanico, The Black*.[183] Mr. Terrell also completed a book on Baja, California, where he gives an account of Estevanico. He also wrote an article for *Desert Magazine* in 1970. Again, Terrell provides a brief account of the "First Black Man in America: Estevanico."[184]

John Upton Terrill's book *Apache Chronicle* also provided an account of Cabeza de Vaca, the "First White man in the American Southwest," and, of course, Estevanico, the "First Black Man in America."[185] Of all the literary figures who have written about our Moroccan slave, John Upton Terrill's work is the best on the man, but by far not the only one.

In fact, pro basketball star Kareem Abdul-Jabbar, with the assistance of writer Alan Steinberg, completed a book in 2000 entitled, *Black Profiles in Courage: A Legacy of African-American Achievement*.[186] This book is important for our purposes because one of the people they feature in the book is Estevanico. And one of the aspects that Abdul-Jabbar and Steinberg mentioned about our Moroccan hero is that he "was probably raised a Muslim and spoke Arabic."[187]

African American military historian Bernie McRae Jr. wrote an essay entitled "Estevanico" for the journal *Lest We Forget*. It includes a sixteen-line poem on our Moroccan hero. The poem gives the flavor of the life of the man from Azemmour. McRae wrote:

Turn back time; this is no modern tale.

Turn back time to the dim and distant days of long ago

Rock back the clock 400 years or more

Across the mighty seas to a warm and sunny shore.

The year fifteen hundred is when we start our story

Picture then slave caravans, a starved and filthy lot.

Six hundred women slaves there were, my mother was
among them

Two months they struggled from Timbuktu, across the
desert fierce and hot.

Slave markets of Morocco, were they not evil too?

A kindly master bought her/she lived there a year.

But served no master very long. She died when I was
born.

And thus begins our narrative, a legend you must hear.

I never knew her loving care in sunny Azamur,

As I grew strong and healthy to face slave life without fear,

'Til freedom was my just reward in the New World far
away.

For I am Estevanico, her son, her golden earring in my ear.

Although Mr. McRae provides a telling narrative, it is mostly fiction. There is no evidence Estevanico was born in Mali, where Timbuktu was located, nor that his mother died in childbirth. It is true that Estevanico was able to achieve freedom in 1536—three years before his death. But there is no evidence he was ever in a slave caravan, which was called a "coffle" in Africa.

It is likely that Estevanico was sold into slavery at a Morocco slave market to the Portuguese and subsequently to the Spanish. But there is little evidence to confirm he had a golden earring, nor that the slave's freedom was thought of as a "reward."

In 1974, the book *Estebanico* was issued by writer Helen Rand Parish. Like other biographies of the Moroccan slave, Parish's work is a thin volume of only 128 pages. In the introduction to the book, Ms.

Parish related that it comes from "new historical discovery," though she does not tell us what the "new" part entails. Some book companies list *Estebanico* as "juvenile fiction."[188]

Another children's book by Jeremie Samuel and illustrated by Carter J. Gaston is entitled, *Do You Know Estevanico? Adventures of the World's Greatest Explorer*.[189] The book was published by the CreateSpace Independent Publishing Platform on June 2, 2016. The narrative is only twenty-four pages, so it does not give a careful account of the life of Estevanico.

A more recent biography on Estevanico was completed by Dennis Herrick entitled *Esteban: The African Slave Who Explored America*. It was published in 2018 by the University of New Mexico Press in Albuquerque. Herrick's book, along with an essay on Estevanico by African American scholar Rayford Logan called "Estevanico," are the sources that claim that the Moroccan slave was given his freedom when Señor Dorantes sold him to Señor Mendoza, the viceroy of New Spain in 1536.

This brings us to some of the places in music where the influence of the life of Moroccan Estevanico may be seen, the topic of the next part of this chapter. A man who calls himself "Professor A.L.I.," an educator and rapper, also often goes by the name "Black Steven," or "Black Stephen," which he relates is a nod to honor "Estevanico the Moor." In the song "Black Steven Speaks" on his album called *Carbon Cycle Diaries*, he mentions Estevanico as if he is speaking in the first person.[190]

Professor A.L.I. as Black Steven, speaking as Estevanico tells us in stanza two of his lyrics:

> I choke ghosts from my past with
> a rope made of ether gas.
> Then I let the evil times pass
> It's clear and only natural that
> Niggas come at you to trap you
> But they will put you assassin in
> Shackles
> If you seek revenge, dig many

Graves
Cause you will be betrayed a
Different number of ways.
Many days are spent plotting and
Planning your revenge.
But let me tell you how it's gonna
End, son.
Cold and lonely, dying slowly
Listening to oldies but ain't got no
Homies.

Two other American rappers have completed tracks devoted to Estevanico. On December 25, 2017, A Band Erased from Time produced an album that included the song "The Ballad of Estevanico." The track is in the deluxe edition and was made by Conq. Inc.

The other rapper is Akae Beka, who, on his *Hail the King*, album has a song simply called "Estevanico." The album was released on March 23, 2019. Beka's real name is Vaughn Benjamin, who was born on St. Croix.

Jazz trumpeter Donald Byrd named the first song on his 1970 album *Electric Byrd* "Estevanico." The album was released on May 15, 1970, and the song in question is a jazz-funk track, or what is sometimes called "ambient, space jazz."

Louis Van Taylor, another jazz saxophonist, and his group, which includes a drummer, a keyboard player and a bass, wrote and performed a tune entitled "Estevanico" throughout much of 2020. The sax solo of the track is divine. There is even a performer who calls himself "Estevanico." Indeed, many of his songs have a Moroccan flavor, including a set called the "Whole Moroccan Songs" from 2017.

Multi-talented American song writer and acoustic guitarist Amy Lowe has a song entitled "Estebanico, the Black" from 2021, whose lyrics tell a straight-forward narrative of the life of our hero from Azemmour.[191]

Estevanico was also honored at the 1940 American Negro Exposition in Chicago. He was included as the subject of one of the thirty-three dioramas honoring prominent African Americans in US history.

Our Moroccan hero also appears as a Conquistador in Paradox Interactive's Europa Universalis event. Thus, Estevanico has entered the modern world of video games and, not surprisingly, as a hero. Another game entitled "Mass Effect 2: MSV Estevanico" is an intergalactic quest game, and again the hero is a Black man dressed in a black space suit. In his quest, his ship becomes damaged, and Estevanico is the only one to repair it.

This brings us to some of the places and items where the Moroccan slave, Estevanico, may be seen to have influenced the areas of art and sculpture in Native-American history and American history in general.

There is a variety of paintings and drawings of Estevanico that are extant. The Granger Historical Picture Archive, for example, features in their collection a pen and black ink drawing of the Morocco hero. He stands shirtless on a mountaintop with a long weapon in his right hand. His right knee is bent, and his left leg is straight. He overlooks a southwestern valley with cacti and mesas. Behind him, on horseback, can be seen a conquistador wearing a Spanish officer's helmet. This image is part of the Texas State Historical Society's collection and can be found there among other materials—both images and text—related to the first Black man in America.

In the statue dedicated to Esteban de Dorantes, included in the monuments by John Houser mentioned earlier, Estevanico, dressed in conquistador clothing, stands erect with a sword in his right hand and in his left a mace as tall as the man. He wears a military hat and tall boots and has an undeniable visage of African features and a full beard. The Esteban de Dorantes statue is in front of the Texas State Capitol in Austin, Texas.

The painting *Estevanico: Moorish Explorer* by TyrannoNija shows the dark-skinned Estevanico in the center, dressed in medieval Islamic attire. The Moroccan slave has a full beard, a sharp nose and bright eyes. The image was produced by *Deviant Art* in 2022.

One of the most recent depictions of Estevanico is a sketch by Gordon C. James that accompanied an article in *The Atlantic* by Annette Gordon-Reed in the June 2021 issue of the magazine. The Black man is shown with an open collar, bushy hair and a full beard. He also wears what appears to be Moorish headwear.

Mr. James was born in Washington, DC, and was chosen in a national search as an illustrator hired to work for Hallmark Cards Inc. He left Hallmark in 2001. Later, he settled in a studio in Spokane, Washington. His illustration of Estevanico is quite evocative, a fine companion to the article by Ms. Gordon-Reed.

The National Library of Portugal in Lisbon has in its collection a Baroque figurative pin or broach of a seated bearded Black man. He wears a red cap and has a sword and a silver Spanish officer's battle helmet under his left arm. A print of this image is owned by Afro-Texas.

Another anonymous depiction of Estevanico is a pen and ink drawing entitled *Cortés, with the Moorish Soldier Estevanico, Entering Mexico*, from the sixteenth century.[192] The drawing shows a triumphant Cortés on horseback and behind him Estevanico, the first Black man in America.

The 1898 painting *Coronado Sets out to the North* by American artist Frederick Remington (1861–1909) portrays Spanish explorer Francisco Vazquez de Coronado on his ill-fated quest in 1540–1541 to find the fabled Seven Cities of Cibola. Coronado's two-year expedition, which included hundreds of Spaniards and Native American helpers and guides, did not find the gold.

*Francisco Vasquez de Coronado Making his Way Across New Mexico*, Frederic Remington, 1905. Oil on canvas. Courtesy of Bridgeman Images.

Another drawing of Estevanico was completed by American artist Sam Patrick around the year 1969. Only a photograph exists of the original sketch. Estevanico wears a wide-brimmed hat and is seated. The photograph is owned by the Miriam Matthews Photograph Collection at UCLA.

Another drawing of Estevanico called *Estevanico 1539* was done by print-maker Marianne L'Heureux. The image is of an erect Estevanico, who appears to be wearing a diaper or a loincloth. He has bushy dark hair and a full beard. The state of New Mexico owns the original oil painting. A copy of the print is now available on eBay. Ms. L'Heureux is a French-Canadian professional artist who now lives in New Mexico where she owns a gallery. The Smithsonian has borrowed Ms. L'Heureux's painting of Estevanico.

This notion of wearing a full beard in this depiction of Estevanico is related to a historical tradition, which does not appear in Al-Quran, the Muslim Holy Book, but does appear in Hadith literature, also called the Sunni, which prescribes that all adult Muslim males should wear full beards from adolescence to death.

Another artistic tradition that was influenced by Estevanico is what is called the *Chakwaina kachina* in the Zuni language, as well as other pueblo tongues in the Southwest of America. The Chakwaina is alternately called "Cha'waina" or "Teakwaina." This tradition still exists among the Hopi, the Zuni and the Keresan Tribes. But it is not found among the Tewa people of New Mexico.[193]

The Chakwaina kachina is a doll that usually depicts an ogre, with ferocious teeth, a black goatee and a black mask with very yellow eyes. Many of the most famous of these objects were made in the mid-twentieth century between 1950 and 1970.

The kachina dolls of today's art market are seen as a bridge between the spiritual realm and the earthly realm and also between Hopis and non-Hopis. Among the Hopi, there are at least two hundred and fifty different kinds, each with its own attributes or qualities. They represent everything from animals to abstract concepts. The kachina Hopi dolls were originally made out of a single piece of cottonwood root.

The Navajo people began carving their own versions of the kachina, adding leather, feathers, beads and even turquoise to the creations. Some of the main versions of the kachina dolls are the eagle, representing power; the wolf, a hunter; and the bear, connected to a power that heals the sick.

Needless to say, the Navajo's version of the kachina—like Estevanico—has attributes of owl feathers, bells and beads, and even pieces of turquoise, that were also connected to the Moroccan slave. These associations among the Navajo surely cannot be an accident.

This artistic tradition is important for our purposes because many in the Southwest claim that the doll is a representative of Estevanico, particularly in his role of medicine man or purveyor of black magic. Some scholars, however, have argued that the tradition of the Chakwaina kachina is much older than the time of Estevanico, which were from 1500 to 1539.

The "Ogre" is another prominent kachina doll. The White Ogre represents the Good. The Black Ogre threatens small children who are naughty. The Black version has often been associated with Estevanico going back to the nineteenth century. The kachina called the "Medicine Man" is said to mix herbs and roots and to give advice that both presents and cures sickness. Because of Estevanico's role as a healer, he is sometimes identified with this figure, especially among the Zuni, Hopi and Navajo.[194]

Many American museums and state historical societies, like Texas, Arizona, New Mexico, Wyoming and Idaho, have pieces of art depicting the Chakwaina kachina, as well as other art collections with substantial holdings regarding the American Southwest.

Since her fictive account of the life of Estevanico in her novel from 2014, Laila Lalami has collected images and representations of the Moroccan slave. Among these images is the illustration in the Granger Collection mentioned earlier, as well as illustrations that appear in José Cisneros' *Cabeza de Vaca and His Three Companions on the Texas Coast.*[195]

The 2013 film *The Mysterious Cities of Gold* has a hero named *Esteban.* The hero is loosely based on the life of Estevanico. There was also a television series by the same name that began in 1983, as well as another film produced in 2007 by Jean Chalopin's company, the Movie Plus Group.

We have examined the book in the collection of the Museum of South Texas History. Three of the illustrations for the volume are of de Vaca resting on his musket that is stuck in the sand, while behind him, the dark-skinned Estevanico can be seen with dark hair and a full beard. He appears to be attending to one of the survivors, presumably from Boat Number Three, mentioned earlier in this study.[196]

In the second depiction from the same book, Estevanico kneels in the surf, while above him, de Vaca stands about to pour water on the Moroccan slave. Perhaps this is a depiction of the baptism of Estevanico and the adoption of his Christian name, "Little Stephen."[197]

Finally, in the third depiction of Estevanico, he stands on what appears to be a lifeboat. He is wearing a white suit with a dark belt and a turban-like head covering. Estevanico's skin is very dark. There is an oar in his right hand and a pistol in his left. A large Spanish ship with three sails can be seen over his right shoulder. The artwork was created by Tats Cru, an artistic endeavor for more than thirty years in The Bronx, New York.

Another book about Cabeza de Vaca and Estevanico called *Castaways* was edited by Enrique Pupo-Walker and translated by Frances M. Lopez-Morillas. It was published by the University of California Press in 1993. In 1968, The Westernlore Press published the first American account of the life of Estevanico entitled *Estevanico, The Black* by John Upton Terrell.

Many other pieces of literature that are extant are also based on the life and times of Estevanico, including:

- Dennis Herrick, *Esteban: The African Slave Who Explored America* (Albuquerque: University of New Mexico Press, 2018).
- Andrés Reséndez, *A Land So Strange: The Epic Journey of Cabeza de Vaca* (New York: Basic Books, 2009).
- Donald E. Chipman and Harriett Denise Joseph, *Notable Men and Women of Spanish Texas* (Austin: University of Texas Press, 1999), 17–18.
- William L. Katz, *The Black West: A Documentary and Pictorial History of the African American Role in the Westward*

*Expansion of the United States* (Garden City: Doubleday, 1971).

- Elizabeth Shepherd, *The Discoveries of Esteban the Black* (New York: Dodd and Mead, 1970), 111–114.
- Carolyn Arrington, *Estevanico: Black Explorer in Spanish Texas* (Austin: Eakin Press, 1986).
- James MacDougald, *The Pánfilo de Narváez Expedition of 1528* (St. Petersburg: Marsden House, 2018).

Another series of paintings of Cabeza de Vaca and his companions was produced by artist Ted DeGrazia (1909–1982). Ettore "Ted" DeGrazia was an American impressionist painter, sculptor, composer, actor, director, designer, architect, jeweler and lithographer. De Grazia's *Cabeza de Vaca* series includes one painting of four dark, emaciated figures, three standing and a darker figure with a full beard—most likely our Moroccan hero, Estevanico.[198]

Another painting in the same series shows the four ship-wrecked survivors picking fruit at the tuna grounds when they were among the Mariames and Yguazes Native Americans. The fruit picking is taken place in a large southwestern cactus field south of present-day San Antonio at the southern-most bend of the Nueces River.[199]

Earlier in the Introductory Essay, we wrote about the massive, sculpted creation of artist John Houser in Austin, Texas. It is a series of sculpted figures all related to various aspects of African American history in Texas. In a series of copper plaques at the base of the Texas African American History Memorial is one legend that describes the particulars of the life of Estevanico.[200]

This legend describes the Moroccan's place of birth, his trans-Atlantic voyage, his coming to Galveston Island in Texas, his service to Viceroy Mendoza, his travels into Arizona and New Mexico, and his murder at the hands of the Zuni Indians in March of 1539. The plaque also hints at the ambiguous nature of why Estevanico was a homicide victim.

The article "Exploring Estevanico" by McKenna Kelley in the *South Tampa Bay Magazine* included a photograph of a bust of Estevanico. The bronze bust shows a clean-shaven Black man with bushy hair and an owl feather attached to the back of his head. The bust is of a handsome and obviously African man who looks to be in his twenties or thirties. The bust is now on loan to the St. Petersburg Museum of History in Florida.[201]

There is also a bust of Álvar Núñez Cabeza de Vaca, one of the other four survivors of the 1527–1528 Narváez expedition to the New World. The artwork was financed by Maria Marmoleja and shows the chest and head of the great Spanish explorer. He wears a battle helmet and an armored covering on his chest and has a full beard. The bust is owned by the Museum at Puerto Iguazu in the Republic of Argentina. There is also a poster version of the piece that was designed by Joe Fox.[202]

There is also an image of Estevanico in an article entitled "Explorers," at the website www.teachertube.com. The slave is dressed in a white tunic, white shirt and what appears to be a black bowtie. In the image, Estevanico has a dark and full beard and something dangling from the back of his head, possibly some sort of stripped scarf or other headdress.

There is an "Estebanico Azemmur" drawing by Japanese anime artist Koukou Kaga, in which Estevanico stands wearing Islamic dress with a spear in his hand as tall as the man. He looks like a Negro warrior with a turban and a full beard. The Kaga drawing of Estevanico and another warrior is now on a wall in the medinah or "Old City" of Azemmour, Morocco. The Koukou Kaga creation was also an important focus in an Azemmour street fair in 2010.

Dr. Robert Goodwin's book *Crossing the Continent 1527–1450: The Story of the First African in American History* includes a photograph of the two Black warriors with large lances in the volume which was published by Harper Perennials in 2009.[203]

A 1936 painting by Aaron Douglas entitled *Into Bondage* is another powerful image that is sometimes associated with Estevanico. It depicts an enslaved African who is bound for the Americas with his head hung low and walking solemnly toward a slave ship on the horizon. Those who identify the picture with Estevanico suggest it is from the period around 1520 to 1522 when the Moroccan was sold into slavery by the Portuguese.

*Into Bondage* by Aaron Douglas. Courtesy of National Gallery of Art. © 2023 Heirs of Aaron Douglas / Licensed by VAGA at Artists Rights Society (ARS), NY

A June 18, 2021, article in *Houstonia* magazine by reporter Emma Schkloven entitled "Looking Deeper at the Massive New Juneteenth Mural in Galveston" refers to a mural in Galveston that tells the narrative of Estevanico, beginning with the shipwreck in 1528 and continuing the story all the way to the Moroccan slave's murder among the Zuni in 1539. The painter(s) of the mural are anonymous.[204]

The Legislative Reference Library of Texas in Austin also owns an illustration of Estevanico called *Estevanico: Black Explorer in Spanish Texas*. It features a Black man hunched down, picking a prickly pear or a cactus from the soil with his extended right hand.

In 1999, the state of Texas established the "Estevanico Society." It is an organization dedicated to the roles that early African Americans played in the state. In fact, the society was established with funds from the group called Afro-Texas.

There is also an hour-long film on the Álvar Núñez Cabeza de Vaca expedition and the life of Estevanico. It is entitled "All the World is Human" and was made in 2001. It is part of the PBS series the *Conquistadors* distributed by PBS Distribution.

In the description that comes along with the film and series, PBS Distribution says:

> Tracing the trials of Álvar Núñez Cabeza
> de Vaca, who was shipwrecked off the Gulf
> Coast of Texas in 1528 and lived among the
> Indians for eight years. This program reveals
> how some early Spanish explorers grew to
> empathize with the plight of Native Ameri-
> cans. Through the writings of Cabeza de Vaca
> and excerpts from the famous arguments of
> Dominican friar, Bartolome de las Casas—
> the first appointed protector of Indians by
> the Spanish Crown in which he debated that
> "Indians are humans," the program explores
> the emergence of a new era of acceptance.
> Cabeza de Vaca became a shaman later in his
> life. Few stories match these for sheer drama,
> endurance, and transformation as this.

Another 2020 film entitled *The Time Machine* is a hybrid documentary by Moroccan filmmaker Tarek Bouraque. The film is set in a past, present and future changing sequence from the time of Estevanico's birth, which Bouraque believes was in 1502, until the present-day in the twenty-first century.

Altogether in our analyses, we identified fifty-four pieces of art in several media and genres inspired by the life of Estevanico of Azemmour: seventeen literary pieces; ten pieces of music, twenty-three paintings and drawings, four films, and several other artworks, including a mural, on a city wall in Azemmour, Morocco, and as a heroic figure in two contemporary video games.

Finally, there is also some mention from Cabeza de Vaca that Estevanico "always carried his rosary." The Spaniard was referring to a string of ninety-nine beads that in Arabic are called *Masbaha*, or in some places *Tasbih*. The fingering of this Muslim "rosary" is to remind the believer to contemplate the ninety-nine names for Allah.[205]

This brings us to Chapter Nine of this study of the life of Estevanico of Azemmour, the first Black man in America, in which we will give an evaluation of the 1539 Cabeza de Vaca mission to Cibola. Did it achieve its goals, and how has the mission subsequently been seen by scholarship?

# IX
## Evaluation of de Niza's 1539 Mission to Cibola

Among the outstanding Negro explorers in the New World was
Estevanico, who opened up New Mexico and Arizona for the
Spaniards. Other Negroes, W. E. B. Du Bois says, "accompanied
DeSoto and one of them stayed among the Indians in Alabama
and became the first settler from the Old World."

—Lerone Bennett Jr., *Before the Mayflower*

From a November 15, 2010, article on the Planetary Science Institute
website, as well as a report from the Associated Press, dated July
12, 2017, we may add some facts about the 1539 Marcos de Niza's
expedition to Cibola beyond what we have said in the Introductory
Essay that began this study of Estevanico.[206] We know from these
sources, for example, that De Niza first came to the Americas in 1531
because of his work as a Franciscan friar. The friar lived and worked in
many places including, Peru; Guatemala; and Culiacán, Mexico.

We also know from these two sources that Viceroy Antonio de
Mendoza sent de Niza and Estevanico north with a third principal, a
priest named Honorato. It may also have been the case that Spanish
scholars and explorers still believed that Mexico was an island and
that, eventually, great seas or oceans would be found to the north and
west. So they ventured north in search of the long-lost Seven Cities of
Gold.[207]

In sixteenth-century Spain, where the Marcos de Niza expedition
began, there were two separate legends or myths, if you will, about a
place called Eldorado and another about the "Seven Cities of Gold," or

"Seven Cities of Cibola." Both of these phenomena were believed by western Europeans in the sixteenth to eighteenth centuries to be exotic repositories of gold. In fact, French writer and philosopher Voltaire, in his celebrated satirical novel *Candide*, published in January of 1759, included a trip to the city of Eldorado in the New World. And, of course, Candide found gold there.

The de Niza expedition, on the other hand, concentrated more on finding the fabled Seven Cities of Gold, which were also rumored to contain vast quantities of gold and other precious metals. One reason for this belief was the gold found among the Incas and Aztecs in Central and South America.

There is no way of knowing how much gold the Spanish took from these Native American civilizations because most of it was immediately melted down in Mexico, or New Spain, or was sent back to Europe to undergo the same process.

Because of these finds of gold among the Incas and Aztecs, the Spanish concluded that there must be similar amounts of precious metal reserves in what would become North America. And thus, was born the legend of the Seven Cities of Cibola, or Seven Cities of Gold, or *Siete Ciudades de Cibola* in Spanish.

These fabled cities were first reported by Álvar Núñez Cabeza de Vaca, who, after being shipwrecked off the coast of Florida in 1528, wandered through what would become northern Mexico and the American Southwest.

Álvar Núñez Cabeza de Vaca and his men. Courtesy of American Antiquarian Society / Bridgeman Images.

Cabeza de Vaca in the Desert. Courtesy of The
Stapleton Collection / Bridgeman Images.

The Spanish explorer Alvar Nuñez Cabeza de Vaca
and his men crossing the American Southwest after
escaping from Indians in 1528. Line engraving,
American, 1880. Courtesy of Granger.

Marcos de Niza (1495–1558) emigrated to the Americas in 1531 with the purpose of exploring new lands for Spain. He served missions in Peru and Guatemala and then was chosen to explore land in North America north of New Spain, the Crown's original name for Mexico. More specifically, Fray Marcos, as he was called, was chosen to lead an expedition to explore lands of the Sonoran Desert in northern Mexico. These lands are now part of the Southwest region of the United States, including parts of Texas, Arizona and New Mexico.

In 1537, Fray Marcos arrived in Mexico City at the request of the viceroy of New Spain, Antonio de Mendoza. De Niza, of course, had been preceded by Cabeza de Vaca and the slave Estevanico. Fray Marcos left Culiacán in March of 1539, crossed southwestern Arizona near present-day Lochiel, then ventured toward Zuni Indian territory and the Seven Cities of Gold.

In September of 1539, Fray Marcos returned to Culiacán after claiming that he only saw Cibola from a distance. He had been the provincial superior of the Franciscan order in Mexico. His expedition of 1539 led Francisco Vazquez de Coronado to make a famous exploration a year later to the Zuni Pueblo in present-day northwest New Mexico. Fray Marcos' trek, however, proved to be a great disappointment. The Seven Cities of Gold was nothing more than seven small pueblos, and no gold was to be found there.

Shortly after the de Niza expedition started, Father Honorato became ill and was forced to turn back to Mexico City. The other two, along with their Indian companions, ventured into the unknown and came upon a city called Vacapa. It was while he was in Vacapa that Marcos de Niza sent Estevanico ahead to scout the way north.[208] Today Vacapa is in the municipality of Ixhuacan de los Reyes in the Mexican state of Veracruz. It is a tiny pueblo with a population of around fifty people.

Estevanico soon sent word back that he had spoken to a group of natives who informed him of the existence of a northern trade center. The name of the place, Estevanico reported, was "Cibola." This made Father de Niza hasten his party to join the Black servant from Morocco. Along the path, the Franciscan met several "native admirers" who accompanied him on his journey to Cibola.[209]

These Indian companions reinforced the idea that a great city existed to the north. But some days later, a few native companions in Estevanico's party came back to de Niza's group, barely alive and bloodied, with news that Estevanico had been murdered. Instead of traveling on, Marcos decided not to continue to the city of Cibola but to get close enough to see it in the distance.

Cabeza de Vaca described Cibola as a "beautiful city," and he observed it from a distance on a ridge above the city. Later, in the first edition of his *Relación*, he described the city as "being bigger than Mexico."[210]

The purpose of this chapter is to speak of and evaluate the 1539 mission of Marcos de Niza's exploration to Cibola in present-day New Mexico. Viceroy Mendoza gave de Niza specific instructions that are still extant. This list contained three principal goals. The main one of these was to find gold, silver and other kinds of wealth among the Seven Cities of Gold.[211]

The second goal that Mendoza gave to Marcos de Niza was to gather information about the coast because the viceroy believed it might have been possible to mount a conquest of the area from the sea. In fact, at the same time, Cortés was already garnering ships and supplies in order to conquer the Aztecs from the sea.

The third and final goal that Senor Mendoza gave Marcos de Niza was for him and Estevanico to report on the land routes, on the peoples, and on the minerals in the land of what would become the southwestern portion of the United States.[212] Marcos de Niza died in disgrace in 1558, for Spain had blamed him for not telling the truth about the wealth of Cibola. But the actual personality of de Niza is not entirely clear. French scholar Bandelier, however, examined the available documents at the time and concluded that de Niza was being truthful about his mission.[213]

Carl Sauer published a thorough analysis of the de Niza mission in his book *The Road to Cibola* in 1932.[214] Henry Wagner published an evaluation of the mission to Cibola in 1934 in the *New Mexico Historical Review*, claiming that Marcos was a complete fraud.[215] In 1940 and 1941, Lansing Bloom attacked the views of both Wagner and Sauer that Marcos did not have sufficient time to reach Cibola.[216]

More recently, in a 1997 study using recent archeological finds, William Hartmann argued that the de Niza mission traveled on traditional trade routes and that the mission was completed successfully.

Some scholars like Cleve Hallenbeck, for example, in his 1949 work, berates de Niza for not following any of the three instructions from the viceroy of New Spain, Senor Mendoza. Hallenbeck claimed that de Niza virtually ignored all of the items on the Mendoza instructions. The Hallenbeck book was called *The Journey of Fray Marcos de Niza*, originally published by the University Press of Dallas in 1949 but was redistributed by the *Arizona 100* celebration and commemoration in January 2012.

There can be little doubt that Marcos did not report as much detail as contemporary scholars might like, but the following conclusions are most probably true about the Marcos de Niza mission from Mexico City to Cibola.

First, it is unlikely that Marcos himself actually got to Cibola. Second, he lied about that telling Mendoza that it was a city "of great wealth." Third, the paths taken by scout Estevanico and later by de Niza were traditional routes in the American Southwest.

One final aspect of Marcos de Niza's expedition is an inscription found in 1922 reported to be a message from the friar. This stone inscription was found on South Mountain in Arizona and was etched into the stone. The message said the following in Spanish:

> Friar Marcos de Niza corona todo el Nuebo Mexico
> a su costa ano de 1539.[217]

An English translation of the text may be rendered this way:

> Friar Marcos de Niza crowned all of New Mexico
> at his expense in the year 1539.[218]

When petroglyph experts tested the stone and its mineral content within the carving, they detected petroleum products, like gasoline, that proved that the stone in question was no more than from the early twentieth century. In other words, the de Niza inscription is a fake, perhaps much like what the Franciscan friar said about Cibola, as well.

This brings us to Chapter Ten, the final section of this study on the life and times of Estevanico, the first black man in America, in which we will describe and discuss some of the major historical significances of the hero from Azemmour. In this chapter, we will attempt to answer the question, "Why is Estevanico historically important?"

# X
# The Historical Significance of Estevanico

In 1538, Estevanico (Little Stephen), a Negro explorer, led an expedition from Mexico and discovered Arizona and New Mexico.

—Lerone Bennett Jr., *Before the Mayflower*

We will end this study on the life of Estevanico by enumerating and then discussing several reasons that the Moroccan slave is historically significant. Already in our analysis, we have suggested that:

1. Estevanico was the first Black man in America.
2. Estevanico was the first Black slave in America.
3. Estevanico was the first Muslim in America.
4. Estevanico was the first Black murder victim in America.
5. Estevanico was one of the first guides for the Europeans to follow.
6. Estevanico learned at least seven or eight of the Native American languages of the Southwest and maybe more.
7. Estevanico participated in the first military engagement in America, one that would eventually kill him.

There are, however, a number of historically relevant implications about his life. We will list several of these and discuss each of them.

1. Estevanico was the first freed Black slave in America in 1536.
2. Estevanico appeared to have been an equal partner in his

party of four men and as important as the other three, who were White.

3.  Estevanico was the first non-Indian to see what is now the state of Arizona.
4.  Estevanico blazed the trail that the Coronado Expedition would follow a year later in 1540.
5.  Estevanico did much to allay the unrest of the Native Americans of Nueva Galicia simply because they trusted and respected him.
6.  In exploring the southern part of what would become the United States, Estevanico walked well over five thousand miles from 1528 until 1539. Today that would be the equivalent of walking from New York to Los Angeles and then two-thirds of the way back.
7.  Estevanico's extraordinary global awareness.

Regarding item number 1, in 1528, Estevanico first stepped on the shores of what would become the United States. That is nearly an entire century before the "twenty or so Negroes" landed in Virginia in August of 1619 and the December 1620 landing at Plymouth Rock in Massachusetts.

In sixteenth-century Spain, from which Marcos de Niza's exploration began, there existed two separate legends or myths, if you will, about a place called Eldorado and another place called the Seven Cities of Gold. In the sixteenth to eighteenth centuries, Western Europeans believed both of these phenomena to be secret repositories of gold in the New World. In fact, in chapter XVII of his celebrated satirical novel *Candide* published in January of 1759, Frenchman Voltaire included the hero's visit to the legendary Eldorado.

On the other hand, the de Niza exploration concentrated on finding the Seven Cities of Gold, which were rumored to contain large quantities of gold, silver and other precious metals and stones. One reason for this belief was the gold found among the Incas and Aztecs in the New World. There is no way of knowing how much gold the Spanish took from the Incas and Aztecs because most of it was immediately melted down in Mexico or sent back to Europe.

These legendary cities were first reported by Alvar Núñez Cabeza de Vaca, who, after being ship-wrecked off the coast of Florida in 1528, wandered through what would become Texas and northern Mexico. When Estevanico did so, that simultaneously made him the first Black man in America, the first Black slave in America, as well as the first Muslim in what would become the United States.

When Estevanico died at the hands of the Zuni people in what would become New Mexico, he also became the first Black murder victim in America. And shortly before that, he was certainly the first Black explorer in the New World, again long before those who came a century later to Comfort, Virginia, in 1619.[219]

In our analyses in Chapter Four, we maintained that Estevanico, in addition to his fluency in Arabic, Portuguese, and the Spanish tongue, he also acquired a facility and competency in at least seven or eight American Indian languages and maybe many more than that.

We have said a great deal about the communication skills, item number 6 in the above list, possessed by Estevanico, but some of the Spaniards who knew him well provide even further insight into this aspect of the Moroccan slave. Before sending the guide off to Cibola, the viceroy of New Spain, Señor Mendoza, referred to the first Black man in America as "*Una persona razon*," or "A person of reason." He meant, of course, a man of reason and discernment.[220]

In Cabeza de Vaca's narrative of his expedition to the north from Mexico City, he observed the following about Estevanico:

> The Black man always spoke to them and informed himself
> about the roads we wished to travel and the villages that there
> were and about other things that we wanted to know.[221]

In another place in his narrative concerning his thoughts about Estevanico, Friar de Niza observed that, "The Black Man acted and survived on his wits." The Franciscan related that Estevanico was the one "who was sent out, alternately into the wilderness and into crowds, playing the crucial and dangerous roles of scout and mediator."[222]

Regarding item 7 listed above, Estevanico and his party participated in the first military skirmish in the New World in the northwest corner of what would become New Mexico.

If some historical sources are correct, then Estevanico was the first Black slave to gain his freedom in America, again a century before slaves like Juan Garrido, Anthony Johnson, and those in Virginia in 1619. Estevanico clearly acted as a buffer between the staid and proper White Europeans and the Native American peoples whose languages he acquired so he could play that role.[223]

In many ways, far more so than Estevanico's three White Spanish compatriots, as evidenced by the fact that the Moroccan slave was given his freedom in 1536 and was thereafter trusted to play equal roles of guide and leader as were assumed by his White companions.

Like the "twenty-odd Negroes in Virginia," the status of Estevanico was not always abundantly clear. He was a slave to Senor Dorantes, but later, he may have been an indentured servant or even a free man, as some historic sources report about his status. In fact, they say he was a free man in the final three years of his life.[224]

In some of the sources about the 1619 Africans brought to Virginia—in Virginia documents themselves—these Africans are referred to as "servants" and even "indentured servants." And a similar question may be raised about the status of Estevanico's in regard, for example, under the viceroy of Mexico, Señor Mendoza, in whose stead the Moroccan slave traveled north after all three White Spanish gentlemen declined to lead the expedition. Perhaps this is the biggest evidence that the figure of Estevanico had an exalted place in the service of Spain at the time of his death.[225]

In the last forty years, several scholars have criticized the philosophical foundations of the 1619 Project and Critical Race Theory by arguing against their univocal insistence that race is the only factor when it comes to identity. Josaphat Bekunuru Kubayanda (1944–1991), a man who was educated on three continents, wrote about the dangers of too narrowly understanding identity in his essay *On Colonial/Imperial Discourse and Contemporary Critical Theory*.[226]

Albert Memmi and his great work, *The Colonizer and the Colonized*, originally published in French in 1957, also offered forceful criticism of concentrating personal identity only on race alone. Yale scholar Rolena Adorno has also made many contributions in regard to the same phenomenon, including the fine essay "Estevanico's Legacy:

Insights into Colonial Latin American Studies from Postcolonial Africa." She says the univocal approach to viewing the life of Estevanico is "misleading if not preposterous."[227] And she is entirely correct about that matter.

The work of Albert Memmi helped to suggest one ought to go beyond the common binary opposition of colonizer and colonized so as to be able to show the common mutual dependence between the two. Memmi's books are harshly against the Marxist-Leninist push—even in American politics—that categorically asserts the claim that Estevanico was nothing more than a Black slave who was oppressed by White Europeans. And they are decidedly incorrect about that.

Perhaps the most significant attribute of the person of Estevanico was his extraordinary global awareness. The Moroccan slave had what might be labeled a "tri-continental" experience of the world, that included North Africa, Europe and the New World. And with each of those worlds also came its own set of myths, symbols and rituals peculiar only to that world.

This tri-continental awareness can best be seen in the symbols that Estevanico employed at the end of his life. If he prayed the morning he was killed, it undoubtedly was to Allah, the God of the Prophet Muhammad. If Estevanico was murdered at dawn, as some sources suggest, and if he prayed at that time, then it would most likely have been the Fajr, which is to be prayed at dawn. The Fajr prayer consists of two rakats or verses. The first of these in Arabic transliteration says *Subhanaka Allahuma wa bihamdika wa tabark as muka wa ta ala jaduka wa ilaha ghairuk.* In English, this may be translated this way: "Glory be to you, oh Allah, and all prayers are due unto You and blessed is your name and high is your majesty and none is worthy of worship but You."

The second rakat of the Fajr prayer tells us this: *Subhaa Allah wa-hamdu liiaah wa laa ilahaa wa AllAAH-HO AKBAR WA LAA HAWLA WA LAHAWLA WAA LA QUWWATA ILLA Billaagh.* This may be rendered in English as "Glory be to Allah, praise be to Allah, there is not god except Allah. Allah is the most great, and there is no power or strength but that of Allah."

Some say the Fajr prayer is the one that Allah loves the most because most people are still asleep at that hour, so He enjoys the silence and the hearing of it prayed by those at sunrise. It is quite possible that Estevanico was aware of the tale and may well have prayed it when he was murdered at the hands of the Zuni people in 1539.

The other four daily prayers of Islam are the Zuhr, said at noon; Asr, in the late afternoon; Maghrib, after sunset; and the Ish, an evening time prayer. These five daily prayers are collectively known in Islam as Salat, the Classical Arabic word for "Prayer." The Moroccan slave's use of the calabaza, or ritual gourd, and its employment as a symbol of healing power and knowledge affected the safe passage of the scouting party from tribe to tribe in the Sonoran Desert.

The Moroccan Arabic word, calabaza is a gourd or squash that is available year-round there. It is also, at times, turned into a magical gourd used in divination, healing, and as a telling of the future. Estevanico and his companions employed the calabaza for exactly these purposes in New Mexico in the early sixteenth century. Because of this, there is little wonder that Estevanico chose to send his "healing gourd" ahead of his party to Cibola in an attempt to replicate the successes he had experienced at other Native American villages and pueblos earlier.

But there was also the third continent and third world—the European world—in which Estevanico was a slave under the direction of White Europeans. In fact, whenever the slave was in the company of the Spaniards, he reassumed his position in the grand scheme of things from the perspective of the Crown of Spain.

One way to see the tri-continental approach to culture in the United States is to refer to a 1931 book by Edwin R. Embree called *Brown America*. Mr. Embree refers to the work of cultural anthropologist Melville J. Herskovits, who states that out of 1,551 Negroes examined by him in Harlem and at Howard University in Washington, DC, one-third of them—or 33 percent—claimed partial American Indian ancestry.[228]

If Dr. Herskovits is correct about this figure, then Estevanico is not alone in his tri-continental perspectives on American culture from the sixteenth century to the present. African, Europe and Native American traditions may well have come together in more American Black people than we previously were fully aware.

And the first Black man in America, who was also the first from this tri-continental perspective, did all of these other activities in the eleven years between 1528 and 1539. The Moroccan slave from Azemmour clearly was a great human being. In many ways on par with American figures like George Washington, Alexander Hamilton, Benjamin Franklin and Abraham Lincoln. And that is wonderful company to be among, indeed.

But we must caution against one thing when it comes to the life of Estevanico. He was, as we have shown, by no means one-dimensional. He was, as we have seen, a slave, a Muslim, an adventurer, a scout or guide, a Moor, an interpreter and translator, an explorer, and, in many ways, an unrecognized conquistador, for—unlike the understanding of the writers of the *New York Times*' "1619 Project," and the teachers of Critical Race Theory, as well, Estevanico was far more than simply being a Black man.[229]

Another 1994 source, a reference work entitled *Historic World Leaders*, published by the Gale Research Project in Detroit, under the entry for "Estevan," or "Stephen" in Portuguese, describes him as a "Heroic Black Explorer." But this unidimensional understanding of Estevanico is misleading, as well as being preposterous under the conditions of slavery that impinged upon his life even when he and the three White Spaniards were together. Estevanico was so much more than being Black.[230]

In fact, another way to see the historical importance of the life of Moroccan slave Estevanico is to see that he is listed among a group of explorers in an article entitled "Ten Great Explorers in History" by Jonathan Gordon. In that essay, Mr. Gordon included our hero in a list along with Leif Erickson, Marco Polo, fourteenth-century Moroccan scholar Ibn Battuta, Christopher Columbus, Ferdinand Magellan, Sacagawea, Francis Drake, Roald Amundsen, and Neil Armstrong. And, above all else, perhaps this is the best way to understand the level of significance the man from Azemmour, Morocco, has had on the history of the United States and the world.[231] In terms of contemporary translations and editions of the *Relación*, Enrique Pena completed a Spanish edition and published it with Wentworth Press in 2018.[232]

This brings us to some comments on the primary sources of the life and times of Moroccan slave Estevanico followed by the Notes of this study, the Bibliography, an appendix on foreign words and phrases, an appendix on the Narváez expedition, and a third appendix on Juan Garrido.

Before all of that, however, we want to add one more discussion about the claim that Estevanico was the first Black man and first Black slave in the United States. We may call this addition an Afterword on the life of Estevanico of Azemmour.

# Afterword on the Life of Estevanico

In this Afterword, we wish to return to the issue that Estevanico was the first Black man and first Black slave in the United States. Earlier in this study, we pointed out that another man named John Garrido may have been the first documented Black man to arrive in the US and may also have been the first Black conquistador. And like the other conquistadors, Garrido soon succumbed to the lure of wealth and fame in the New World.

We can be certain that Juan Garrido joined Diego Velázquez de Cuéllar and the legendary Juan Ponce de Leon in the colonization of Cuba and Puerto Rico, respectively. Then, in 1513, he joined Ponce de Leon's well-known expedition in search of the fountain of youth in Florida. That date of 1513 is fifteen years before Estevanico's arrival to America in 1528 with the Narváez expedition that began in 1527.[233]

Thus, some are quick to romanticize Juan Garrido as Estevanico has been. But several facts about Garrido suggest that this would not be a wise thing to do. For one thing, Garrido, like the other conquistadors, was no saint in the ways that Estevanico clearly was. For one thing, Garrido participated in Hernán Cortés' destruction of the Aztec people, along with one hundred thousand Tlaxcalan allies. Thus, Juan Garrido is to be numbered among the oppressors, not the oppressed.[234]

Juan Garrido settled in Mexico City in 1524 and left just before the arrival of the Narváez expedition in 1528. Garrido then began a gold mining operation, but he used slave labor to mine the gold.[235] Again, this is an indication that Garrido was among the oppressors. Later, Juan Garrido joined Cortés in the 1530s for yet another expedition, this time into Southern California, in what was called the mythic search for the "Black Amazons." Juan Garrido was rewarded for his service with Cortés, mostly with land and royal positions, But Garrido was an oppressor, and Estevanico was to be numbered among the oppressed.[236]

In a January 7, 2015, article by *Washington Post* reporter Meg Smith entitled "African-American Men: Moments in History From Colonial Times to the Present," she attempts to pinpoint the first Black man in America, and her choice was Columbus' Pedro Alonso Niño, on the Italian's first voyage in 1492.[237] Ms. Smith, however, said nothing about the spotty record of establishing evidence for Pedro Niño and his two brothers who, supposedly, were also part of the crew of the *Nina*, *Pinta* and *Santa Maria*.

In her 2015 article, Ms. Smith then jumps rather abruptly to the year 1623 and the birth of William Tucker, the first recorded birth of a slave in the continental United States mentioned earlier in this study. In making this abrupt jump, however, the *Post* reporter left out Estevanico, Juan Garrido, Antonio or Anthony Johnson, and a Black woman we did not mention earlier. Her name was Zipporah Potter Atkins, born on July 4, 1645.[238]

Ms. Atkins was important for a lot of reasons, but she does not appear on the list of firsts assembled by Meg Smith. One reason that Zipporah Adkins is important is that she was the first Black woman to own land in Boston. So in terms of looking for African-American firsts, the name of Zipporah Potter Adkins should be added to the list of those firsts, along with Juan Garrido, Anthony Johnson, William Tucker, and many others.

On May 20, 2014, Governor Deval Patrick—the first Black governor of Massachusetts—unveiled a plaque during a ceremony to honor Zipporah Potter Atkins, the first Black person to purchase property in Boston. She was only twenty-five years old when she bought the property in 1670, which she held until 1699. Because of a 1641 law, Black children born to slaves were considered free at birth.

Ms. Atkins is believed to be interred at the Copps Hill Burial Ground Cemetery, but to this day, the location of the grave is unknown. The name Zipporah is a Classical Hebrew name. In the Hebrew Bible, or Old Testament, Zipporah was a wife of Moses given to him in marriage by her Midianite priest father. Later, she heroically saved Moses' life and her son's from a random attack from an angel by cutting off her son's foreskin.[239]

Zipporah's explanation for her act is not clear. She is, however, seen as fiercely devoted to her husband, Moses, even though he often neglected her because she was a Midianite. After Moses killed an Egyptian, he fled from the Pharoah and then settled among the Midianites, an Arab people who occupied desert areas in southern Transjordan, or northern Arabia, and the Sinai Peninsula.

Ms. Smith's article did mention, however, two other early Black men in America. One named Mattheus de Sousa and the other, Lucas Santomee. The former came to Maryland in 1634 and was elected to the Maryland General Assembly in 1641. We have written about Mr. de Sousa extensively. He came to the Chesapeake Bay area as an indentured servant. Mr. De Souza also was elected to the Maryland General Assembly in 1641, after his time of indenture had been served.[240]

Lucas Santomee, a Black physician, was also a landowner in what was to become New York City. The Dutch government granted Dr. Santomee a tract of land that stretched from what today is Greenwich Village all the way to Brooklyn. Dr. Santomee attended Yale Medical School, the first Black man to do so.[241]

One reason that de Sousa and Santomee were important for our purposes is that they both appear to have been Black Muslims, but more than a century later than the arrival of Estevanico to North America in 1528.[242]

One final seventeenth-century and early eighteenth-century Black man in America was the slave of the Rev. Cotton Mather in Massachusetts. He called his slave *Onesimus* and became the slave of Mather in 1706, but it appears he was born on the West Coast of Africa in the late seventeenth century.[243]

Onesimus is important for American history because he saved the city of Boston from a smallpox epidemic that ravaged the city in 1721. Onesimus had the idea of exposing healthy people to small amounts of pus from smallpox sores of patients suffering from the disease. Onesimus reasoned that healthy people would get sick but not as sick as a full-fledged attack of the illness. In addition, it turns out that those with the pus exposure had life-long immunity to the disease.

Onesimus soon taught his techniques to the Rev. Mather and a Boston physician named Zabdiel Boylston, who immediately put

Onesimus' theory into practice. Thus was born the idea of immunization in America. On June 26, 1721, Dr. Boylston inoculated his thirteen-year-old son with the controversial smallpox vaccine. Later, in the summer and fall of 1721, the Boston doctor inoculated another 180 to 250 Bostonians. By the middle of the eighteenth century, the Onesimus/Boylston theory was fully accepted in the national medical community.[244]

Mather's slave Onesimus appears to have had many things in common with Señor Dorantes' Estevanico. One of the most important of those is what the Massachusetts minister said about Onesmus in a letter dated July 12, 1716, when he observed, "He is a pretty intelligent fellow."[245]

In her *Post* article, Ms. Smith does include a number of other "firsts" in regard to Black Americans, including Alexander Lucius Twilight as the first African American to graduate from college in America in 1828, and Oberlin College's decision in 1835—two years after its founding—to admit students regardless of their race, and the 1712 passing of a law in South Carolina regarding the handling of runaway slaves in slave states, most of which soon followed South Carolina.

Finally, given today's emphasis in the United States to see race and gender as the only factors for determining personal identity, there is a proliferation of evidence that Estevanico was not simply seen that way by his contemporaries—particularly by Viceroy Mendoza and Friar de Niza. In view of his contemporary sixteenth-century comrades—at least after 1536—Estevanico was seen as a linguist, a scout, a mediator between the Spaniards and the Native Americans, and lastly, as a freed Black man—the first in America.

This, of course, like the lives of Juan Garrido and Anthony Johnson, the life of Estevanico from Azemmour, Morocco, above all else, flies in the face of the twenty-first-century dichotomy of oppressor and oppressed, and Estevanico was numbered among the oppressed.

In his recent book, *The Other Slavery*, about the slavery of Native Americans beginning in the fifteenth century and continuing to the nineteenth century, Andrés Reséndez put both identity by race and the dichotomy of oppressors and oppressed in the crosshairs of his scholarly weapon. He wrote the following about Native American slavery that began long before 1619:

This is not a story in which we have guilty parties and victims. It's a story about human nature, economic rationale, and a harsh environment... This is a story far less about genetics and far more about greed than some will now tell you.[246]

In these two short comments, Professor Reséndez reveals the lie of both the oppressor/oppressed Marxist dichotomy, as well as the idea that slavery was fundamentally about genetics and race.

The bottom line for this Afterword is a very simple one. We stand by our original suggestion at the outset of this study that Estevanico of Azemmour, Morocco, was the first Black man, the first Black slave, and the first freed Black man in the United States.

More recent scholars also have begun to claim that Estevanico of Azemmour was the first Black man in America, including Helen Rand Parish in her 1974 biography, Dennis Herrick in his 2018 book *Esteban: The African Slave Who Explored America*, and James MacDougald and his book entitled *The Pánfilo de Narváez Expedition of 1528: Highlights of the Expedition and Determination of the Landing Place*, published in St. Petersburg, Florida by Marsden House in 2018. So, this author is not alone in the claim.

This brings us to a discussion of the primary sources for this study.

# Notes on the Primary Sources of this Study

The three European survivors of the Narváez expedition wrote a joint report for the Spanish Crown that is no longer extant. Oviedo, however, published it in the third volume of his *Historia General y Natural de las Indias*. Cabeza de Vaca's account is also given in his letter to the Audiencia of Santo Domingo. There are only slight differences between this letter and the *Relación*, which was first published in Zamora, Spain, in 1542.[247]

Similarly, there are only slight differences between the 1542 edition and the 1555 edition of the *Relación*, which was published in Valladolid, Spain. In 1556, Italian Giovanni Battista Ramusio published a fairly accurate account of the *Relación* in Venice. The volume appeared in Ramusio's *Terzo Volume delle Navigationi et Viaggi*. The Englishman Samuel Purchas collected a slightly abridged version of the Ramusio in his *Purchas His Pilgrimes: in Five Bookes*, published in London in 1625.[248]

French scholar Henri Ternaux-Compans translated the 1555 edition of the *Relación* in the seventh volume of his *Voyages, Relations, et Memories*, published in Paris in 1837.[249] The 1555 edition also was published by Buckingham Smith in Washington, DC, in 1851. It was not until 1905 that Mrs. Fanny Bandelier completed an American English version.[250]

More contemporary translations and editions of de Vaca's narrative include a Spanish edition by Enrique Pena, published by Wentworth Press in 2018.[251] Martin A. Favata, with the Arte Publico Press, published an English version in 2001.[252] And the lengthiest account of the de Vaca narrative comes from David Carson's 295-page version with copious notes. It was published by Living Waters Specialties in 2018.[253]

The letter of Viceroy Mendoza of New Spain to Spain on December 10, 1537, has also been frequently printed in both Spanish and English editions.[254] Generic Books published Mendoza'a letters in a 2019 edition. In his biography of Mendoza, Arthur Scott Aiton wrote about the letter in question.[255] The Southern Methodist University Press also published the *Documents of the Coronado Expedition* in 2015. The most important source for the Coronado exhibit remains the *Relación* of Pedro de Castañeda Najera.[256] George Parker Winship published the Spanish text of a 1596 copy that is now owned by the New York City Public Library and available to scholars.[257]

Other sources for the life of Estevanico include Hernando de Alarcón's *Relación* in the fourth volume of his *Documentos Ineditos*.[258] Coronado's letter of August 3, 1540, to Mendoza may be found in Captain Juan Jaramillo in the same work.[259]

Cleve Hallenbeck's *The Journey of Fray Marcos de Niza* was published by Southern Methodist University Press in 1987. It has been a very helpful volume in making sense of the life of Estevanico.[260]

# Appendix A
# Foreign Words and Phrases

In this study of Estevanico, we have employed the following foreign words and phrases in about fifteen to twenty languages. In each item of the list below, we have indicated a foreign word or phrase, as well as the language with which the word or phrase is associated, according to the following key:

- Arabic (Arb)
- Classical Greek (CG)
- French (Fr)
- German (Ger)
- Hebrew (Heb)
- Italian (Ital)
- Koine Greek (KG)
- Latin (Lt)
- Native American Languages (NAL)
- Portuguese (Por)
- Punic (P)
- Spanish (Sp)

These include words in *Ashiwi*, the Zuni language; Avarveres; *Kolhu walawa*; *Maliacones*; *Meriame*; *Albadaos,* and Co, among others. Altogether, then, we have used words and phrases from these seventeen different tongues. There is sufficient evidence that Estevanico of Azemmour, Morocco, learned all of these Native-American languages, plus various forms of sign language.

## Alphabetical List of Foreign Words and Phrases

| | | |
|---|---|---|
| *Aak'u* | Native American dialect. | (NAL) |
| *Abadaos* | Native American tribe. | (NAL) |
| *Abd Ar-Rahman* | Muslim leader. | (Arb) |
| *Rabbi Adibe* | Moroccan Jewish leader. | (Heb) |
| *Alhambra* | Palace Fortress in Granada, Spain. | (Sp) |
| *Alhambra Decree* | Another name for 1492 "Edict of Expulsion." | (Sp) |
| *Al-Malik* | Muslim leader. | (Arb) |
| *Sultan Almoravid* | Eleventh-century Muslim leader. | (Arb) |
| *Al-Maghrib* | Another name for Iberia. Means "Far West" in Arabic. | (Arb) |
| *Altamira* | City in Spain with famous caves. | (Sp) |
| *Al-Andalus* | Another name for Iberian Peninsula. | (Sp/Por) |
| *Ashiwi* | Proper name of Zuni Tribe. | (NAL) |
| *Aitho* | Greek for "Black." | (CG) |
| *Aithiops* | New Testament Greek for "scorched skin." | (KG) |
| *Al-Jaidada* | Moroccan city also called *Mazegon*. | (Arb) |

| Almohids | Muslim dynasty. | (Arb) |
|---|---|---|
| Antonio | "Anthony" | (Por) |
| Auto da Fe | "Act of Faith" in Portuguese, related to the Inquisition and to "burning at the stake." | (Por) |
| Averroes | Latin name for *Ibn Rushd*. | (Arb) |
| Azama | Olive tree in Punic. | (P) |
| Azambo | Punic name for "Azemmour." | (P) |
| Azemmour | City in Morocco where Estevanico was born. | (Por) |
| Andres Azoulay | Jewish advisor to King Mohamed VI of Morocco. | (Arb) |
| King Boabdil | Final Muslim king in Granada, fifteenth century. | (Arb) |
| Lalla Aivha Bahriya | One of Morocco's "three saints." | (Arb) |
| Barghanantes | Berber dynasty. | (P) |
| Barbarosa | Muslim Pirate. | (Arb) |
| Bigotes | Whiskers" in Spanish. | (Sp) |
| Calavazza | Gourd | (Arb) |
| Calique | Spanish for the "boss." | (Sp) |
| Callabezza | Gourd | (Por), (Sp) |
| Carvela | Name for small pirate ship. | (Por) |

| | | |
|---|---|---|
| *Ceuta* | A pueblo in Mexico. | (Sp) |
| *Cevola* | Coronado's name for Cibola. | (Sp) |
| *Chiuahu* | State of Mexico. | (Sp) |
| *Chakiwina* | Native American doll. | (NAL) |
| *Chilixi-calli* | Pueblo in Choluli province of Mexico. | (Sp) |
| *Cibola* | City of "Seven Cities of Gold." | (Sp) |
| *Cicuyw* | Former name of Pecos Valley. | (Sp) |
| *Culiacán* | City in Mexico. | (Sp) |
| *Dar El-Baroud* | Tower in Kasbah in Morocco. | (Arb) |
| Daro | River in southern Spain. | (Sp) |
| *Doukkail* | Name of Punic Tribe in Morocco. | (P) |
| *Esteban* | "Stephen" | (Sp) |
| *Esteban negro* | "Black Stephen" | (Sp) |
| *Estevanico* | "Little Stephen" | (Por) |
| *Estevan* | Stephen | (Por) |
| *Fez* | Imperial city of Morocco. Home of the world's oldest university. | (Arb) |

| Fusco | Means "dark." | (Por) |
|---|---|---|
| Geniu | River in Southern Spain. | (Sp) |
| Hajj | Muslim pilgrimage requirement. | (Arb) |
| Haouzig | Pueblo in Mexico. | (Sp) |
| King Hasan II | Moroccan king. | (Arb) |
| Hawikuh | Another name for Cibola. | (NAL) |
| Hopi | Native American tribe. | (NAL) |
| Horro | Free man in early Portuguese. | (Por) |
| Ifrigaya | Another name for Tunisia. | (Arb) |
| Moulay Ighi | Muslim saint buried in the Atlas Mountains. | (Arb) |
| Infante Dom Henrique | "Henry the navigator." | (Por) |
| Isidore of Seville | (560–636) Early church father | (Sp) |
| Isle of Mahaldo | "Island of Misfortune," de Vaca's name for Galveston Island. | (Sp) |
| Ixhuacan | City in Veracruz, Mexico. | (Sp) |
| Rey Jao | King John I of Portugal. | (Por) |
| Jeradi | Province in Morocco. | (Arb) |
| Jerez de la frarerno | City in Spain. | (Sp) |
| Kasbah | Coastal city of Algeria. | (Arb) |

| *Kawaiki* | Native American dialect. | (NAL) |
|---|---|---|
| *Keres* | Family of Native American languages. | (NAL) |
| *Keresan* | Native American tribe. | (NAL) |
| *Khair ad-Din* | Ottoman ruler (1478–1546). Barbarosa's real name. | (Arb) |
| *Khairouan* | Umayyad dynasty capital. | (Arb) |
| *Kiva* | Native American dwelling. | (NAL) |
| *Kolhu walawa* | Zuni Heaven. | (NAL) |
| *Las Naffrigos* | The "ship-wrecked." | (Sp) |
| *Lashbuna* | Another name for "Lisbon." | (Por) |
| *Abdallah Laroui* | Azemmour native and philosopher. | (Arb) |
| *Lasaux* | City in France with ancient caves. | (Fr) |
| *Ma'ad* | Another word for Day of Judgment. | (Arb) |
| *Ma'l Oyattski'I* | Salt Mother in Zuni culture. | (NAL) |
| *Malaga* | Port city in southern Spain. | (Sp) |
| *Maliacones* | Native American tribe. | (NAL) |

| Mathando | "Island of Misfortune." Spanish name for Galveston Island, in Texas. | (Sp) |
|---|---|---|
| Mala'ika | Angels. | (Arb) |
| Mariames | Native-American tribe. | (NAL) |
| Marrakesh | City in Morocco. | (Arb) |
| Mauros/mauroi | Black or dark. | (CG) |
| Masaba | Muslim rosary. | (Arb) |
| Matagordo Bay | Fishing spot in Texas. | (Eng) |
| Maysari al-matsuri | Muslim leader. | (Arb) |
| Mazayin | City in Morocco. | (Arb) |
| Medinah | Arabic word for "city." | (Arb) |
| Mellah | Jewish quarter of a city. | (Heb) |
| Meriame | Native American tribe. | (NAL) |
| Miaara | Jewish cemetery in Morocco. | (Heb) |
| Moguer | City in southern Spain. | (Sp) |
| Moulay Zayam | Muslim Moroccan leader. | (Arb) |
| Muhammad | Prophet of Islam. | (Arb) |
| Musa Ibn Nusayr | Muslim leader. | (Arb) |
| Mustapha | Arabic for "Stephen." | (Arb) |
| Nabiim | Prophets | (Arb) |

| *Niger* | Black | (Lt) |
|---|---|---|
| *Nina* | Ship of Columbus. | (Ital) |
| *Nubuwwah* | Another word for prophets. | (Arb) |
| *Nueces* | River in Texas. | (Sp) |
| *Ou es-ribi* | River in Morocco. | (Fr) |
| *Pedro Alonso Niño* | Columbus Black navigator. | (Sp) |
| *Perpetual Rey* | "Eternal king." | (Lt) |
| *Pinta* | Columbus ship. | (Ital) |
| *La Purisima Concepcion* | Mission church erected by Coronado. | (Sp) |
| *Probenza* | Name of essay by Juan Garrido. | (Sp) |
| *Qadar* | Divine Decree in Islam. | (Arb) |
| *Qabil Ibn Nafi* | Muslim general. | (Arb) |
| *Querrecho* | Another name for the Apache Indians. | (NAL) |
| *Qutab* | Books | (Arb) |
| *Rabbi Solomon Reuveni* | Jewish leader of Azemmour | (Heb) |
| *Rabbi Pinchus Synagogue* | House of worship in Morocco. | (Heb) |
| *Ramadan/Ramatana* | Islam's month of fasting. | (Arb) |
| *Relación* | Work by Cabeza de Vaca. | (Sp) |
| *Rue Talmud Torah* | Street in Morocco. | (Fr) |

| | | |
|---|---|---|
| *Saadian* | South Moroccan dynasty. | (Arb) |
| *Salat* | Muslim requirement for "Prayer." | (Arb) |
| *Roberto di San Severino* (1418–1487) | Italian Count di Colorno. | (Ital) |
| *Santa Maria* | Columbus ship. | (Ital) |
| *Sawm* | Another name for Ramadan or fasting. | (Arb) |
| *Seville* | City in Spain. | (Sp) |
| *Shahadah* | Muslim profession of faith. | (Arb) |
| *Shiwi* | Name of Zuni language. | (NAL) |
| *Sinoloa* | Native American tribe. | (NAL) |
| *Sidi Ouadoud* | Lighthouse in Morocco. | (Arb) |
| *Sonora* | Native American tribe who lived in the desert. | (Sp) |
| *Souk* | "Market" in Classical Arabic. | (Arb) |
| *Stacona/Stadaconi/ kanada* | Early names for "Canada." | (NAL) |
| *Tawhid* | The Oneness of Allah. | (Arb) |
| Tangiers | Seaport in North Morocco. | (Arb) |
| *Tashbih* | Another name for *masaba*. | (Arb) |
| *Tlaxcala* | Mexico's smallest state. | (Sp) |
| *Fray Marcos de Niza corona todos el nuevo Mexico a su sustra ano 1539.* | "Father Marcos de Niza crowns all of New Mexico at his expense in 1539." | (Sp) |
| *Umayyad* | Islamic dynasty. | (Arb) |

| *Vacapa* | Pueblo near Veracruz, Mexico. | (Sp) |
|---|---|---|
| *Walkulla* | River in Florida panhandle. | (NAL) |
| *Wallawa* | Another name for Zuni Heaven. | (NAL) |
| *Wanderlust* | Wonderlust | (Ger) |
| *Wattasid* | Muslim dynasty. | (Arb) |
| *Wizeyah* | Name of South American oil company. | (Arb) |
| *Yaum al-Qiyamah* | Day of Judgment. | (Arb) |
| *Yguazes* | Native American tribe. | (NAL) |
| *Zakat* | Muslim requirement for Almsgiving. | (Arb) |
| *Zaoulia of Telouet* | Capital of French Protectorate in Morocco. | (Fr/Arb) |
| *Zipporah* | Wife of Moses. | (Heb) |

# Appendix B
# Narváez Expedition: 1527 to 1528 and the Ships He Used

In December of 1526, Spanish nobleman Pánfilo de Narváez was given a title to all of the lands between the Rio de la Palmas and the Cape of Florida by the king of Spain. His subsequent voyage to the New World consisted of five ships and a crew of about six hundred. These included men from Spain, Portugal, Greece and Italy, among other nations. The Narváez fleet left Spain on June 17, 1527.

The Narváez expedition arrived at Santo Domingo in what is now the capital city of the Dominican Republic, but in the early sixteenth century, was known as Hispaniola. In Santo Domingo, 140 sailors deserted the expedition. Afterward, the expedition sailed to Cuba, where a hurricane sank two of Narváez's ships and killed fifty men and many of the expedition's horses.

Narváez's expedition remained in Cuba until late February of 1528, at which time the Spanish ships carrying four hundred remaining sailors sailed to a region that today would be Tampa Bay, Florida. After claiming the land for Spain, Narváez began an overland expedition in 1528 with about three hundred men. The trek northward was difficult. They had to fight Indians, and there was a lack of food and new diseases. Eventually, Navarez and his men reached the area of present-day Saint Marks, Florida, sometime at the end of July 1528.

Pánfilo de Narváez (ca. 1480–1528) and his
companions reach the Gulf of Mexico after crossing
Florida, 1528. Wood engraving, nineteenth century.
Courtesy of Granger.

The remaining ships of the larger expedition failed to come to the aid of those who trekked to the north. Narváez's men constructed five more vessels that were more like rafts than ships. In late September 1528, two hundred and forty-five men sailed along the Florida coast with the hope of reaching Mexico, or what was then called New Spain.

These five rafts drifted along the northern part of the Gulf of Mexico, passing Pensacola, Florida, as well as the mouth of the

Mississippi River. By early November 1528, the rafts were gradually lost, including the one that carried Narváez, out to sea. Of the original six hundred men, only four survived, three Spaniards and the Moroccan slave Estevanico.

When the rafts were drifting, they sailed haltingly along the coasts of Alabama, Mississippi, Louisiana and Texas. Finally, the only surviving boat landed at a place the four survivors named the "Island of Misfortune," that most likely was the island of Galveston, Texas.

From 1529 until 1534, Cabeza de Vaca and his companions—including two other Spaniards and Estevanico—lived a meager life among the Karankawa Indians, in a state of semi-slavery and often separated from each other so they would not devise a scheme for escape.

In this time with the Karankawa, Cabeza de Vaca also began to utilize the slight medical skills he had acquired and began to play the role of a healer. In 1534, he and the other survivors—Alfonso de Castillo, Andres Dorantes, and the Moroccan slave Estevanico—started to walk west across Texas and into Mexico. With the help of many Native Americans along the way, peoples whose languages Estevanico had learned, the group eventually crossed the Pecos and Colorado Rivers, making their way toward the Spanish outposts. Along the way, the entire trip was recorded by Cabeza de Vaca in his *Relación*.

In April 1536, a Spanish slaving party found the four Narváez survivors. A short time later, they were taken to Mexico City of New Spain. In 1537, Cabeza de Vaca returned to Spain, where he expressed outrage at the Spanish treatment of the Native Americans. Later, he was charged with malfeasance and was finally pardoned in 1552. At the end of his life, de Vaca became a judge in Seville, Spain, where he died in 1557.

Before the sixteenth century, European battleships were powered—as they had been from ancient times—by oars and oarsmen. In the late fifteenth and early sixteenth centuries, European navies entered what could only be called the "Age of the Sail." The largest of Spanish and English ships was known as the "galleon." These were large, multi-decked sailing ships used as armed cargo carriers.

These galleons usually had three or more masts and as many as eight to ten large sails attached to those masts. One British galleon, for example, sported four masts that included the tallest of mainmast;

the second tallest or foremast; the mizzenmast, typically shorter than the first two; and the bonaventure mizzenmast that typically was a lateen-rigged mast, often the shortest of the four. A British galleon thus described would also have included six to ten main sails, usually four large ones on the mainmast and foremast and four or five on the smaller masts.

It is likely that the ships that sailed to the New World in the Narváez expedition were versions of the Spanish galleon. Another important feature of the Spanish galleon was its ability to carry many cannons to engage in warfare. Typically, the galleon had cannons mounted on its sides, as well as three to six arms attached to the rear of the craft. These rear arms usually included what the British called the "culverin," the "demi-culverin" and the "minion."

The culverin was a long-range, ship-killing cannon—a brass muzzle-loader. The demi-culverin was also a long-range brass muzzle-loader that could fire eight shots a minute. The minion was a smaller weapon capable of penetrating the bulwarks of the upper decks of enemy ships.

Additionally, both the British and Spanish galleons were equipped with cannons mounted on both the starboard and port sides of the vessel, from aft to stern. Typically, the galleon had four cannons on both sides, bringing the grand total to eleven cannons on each of the British and Spanish galleons. Thus, in all, the Narváez expedition most likely included forty cannons as well as long guns and pistols.

These galleons of the early sixteenth century were typically one hundred to one hundred and fifty feet long and fifty feet wide. The preferred ratio was 3:1 or even 4:1 if the proper wood was available. Spanish galleons were made on the Basque coast of Spain, as well as in Havana and in the Philippines. The wood of choice in Europe was oak; in Havana, mahogany; and in the Philippines, various other hardwoods.

We know nothing about what chores Estevanico was given as a sailor. It is likely that most of what he did on-ship was to cater to his owner, Señor Andres Dorantes de Carranza, but he may have had seaman duties, as well. We do know, however, that it was the custom for slaves and servants to sleep on any available space on the main deck.

In addition to the galleon, the Spanish also used two other kinds of crafts in its sixteenth-century navy. The caravel and the carrack. The former was a medium-sized ship with a shallow draft and lateen, or triangular sails. They were fast, easy to maneuver and only required a small crew. It is likely that the main ship of Narváez was a galleon and the remaining ships were of the caravel variety. The two most famous caravels to arrive in the New World were Columbus' *Nina* and the *Pinta*. The largest of the Columbus ships was the *Santa Maria*, which was a galleon.

It is also possible that Narváez's other crafts, besides the main ship, were of the carrack kind. The carrack, or *nao*, was developed in the fifteenth century by the Portuguese. They were generally three or four-masted crafts for use in the Atlantic Ocean. The carrack also became widely used by European maritime powers.

The carrack had a high, rounded stern with a large aftcastle, forecastle, and bowsprit at the stern. The carrack began to be deployed by the Spanish in the early sixteenth century to explore and map the New World. The Spanish carrack was usually square-rigged on the foremast and the mainmast and lateen-rigged on the mizzenmast. The Spanish called their version of the carrack the *nao*.

There are no records of the nature and style of Narváez's fleet, but it is likely that his main ship was a galleon, and his other crafts were either of the carrack or the caravel variety of Spanish ships.

# Appendix C
# Juan Garrido as the First Black Man in America

I was the first to experiment with sowing wheat in new Spain...
and I did this... at my own expense.

—Juan Garrido, "La Probanza"

## Introduction

The purpose of this final appendix is to make some remarks on why I have not chosen Juan Garrido to be the first African in America. The claim would seem to make sense. Like Estevanico, Garrido was born in West Africa, but thirteen years before Estevanico. Like the Moroccan, Garrido spent time in Portugal and sailed under the Spanish Crown. It is likely that Garrido was born in the Kingdom of Kongo, present-day Angola and the Democratic Republic of the Congo.

As did Estevanico, Garrido first stepped on American soil in what would become Florida, but he did it in 1513, fifteen years before the Moroccan slave would do the same. Juan Garrido was involved in the conquest of Mexico and, in fact, retired to Mexico City at the end of his life with his wife and three children.

Juan Garrido also took part in the Spanish gold rush in the Zacatula province of what is now Baja, California. While hoping to find gold pearls and Amazons, Garrido and his company only found Native Americans, disease and poor weather. The expedition, consequently, was a failure, and that is when he returned to Mexico City, where he died sometime between 1547 and 1550.

It is clear that from these facts, Juan Garrido entered what would later become the United States fifteen years before Estevanico of Azemmour. Nevertheless, we still maintain that Estevanico should be given the honor of being the first Black man in America. There are several reasons for making this claim.

First, although Estevanico received his freedom from the Spanish in 1536 and appeared to have lived his final three years as a freedman, several scholars, such as Peter Gerhard, who wrote an essay in the *Hispanic American Historical Review* from 1978, suggested that Juan Garrido was among a group of "black freedmen from Seville and elsewhere who found passage in westward-bound ships."[261] Dr. Gerhard quotes Ruth Pike, another early Spanish-era scholar who made the same claim about Señor Garrido.[262]

A second reason for believing that Estevanico should be given the honor of the first Black man in America is that when Garrido came as a freedman in 1513, he was seen as part of the Spanish authorities, and thus in Marxist terms, he was part of the oppressors rather than the oppressed. Our Moroccan hero, on the other hand, came as a slave of Senor Andrés Dorantes de Carranza and later was sold or was given to the first governor of New Spain, who sent the slave on the expedition that would kill him to northwest New Mexico in 1539.

A third reason for favoring Estevanico as the first Black Man in America is that the expeditions he conducted in the continental US were much more extensive than those of Juan Garrido. The Moroccan walked thousands of miles in his explorations of America, while Juan Garrido did not.

It is also quite clear that Estevanico's intellectual abilities were far superior to those of Señor Garrido's. There is no indication, for example, that Garrido acquired any of the native languages of the native people he met, while the Azemmour slave spoke at least seven of them fluently.

It is true that Juan Garrido was the first African-European to introduce the cultivation of wheat in what would become the United States. He also held a number of political posts under the Spanish Crown. Garrido's only surviving writing was his "Probanza," from which we have used one line for the epigraph of this appendix. But this work was written and published in September of 1538, while Cabeza de Vaca's narrative, which included many remarks about Estevanico, was written beginning in 1527 and published in 1542.

If we add to the fact that Juan Garrido participated in Hernán Cortés's destruction of the Aztec people, along with one hundred thousand Tlaxcalan allies, and thus Garrido is to be numbered among the oppressors in terms of the contemporary Neo-Marxists, and not the oppressed of which Estevanico was a member, at least until 1536 when he became a freedman.

Thus, our conclusion to this appendix should be clear, Estevanico of Azemmour, Morocco, is a better moral and intellectual choice as the first Black man in America, even though Juan Garrido was there before him.

# Appendix D
# Estevanico and His Tri-Continental Life

One final way to understand the life of Estevanico of Azemmour is to make some observations about the Moroccan's "tri-continental" life. He was, as we have shown, born in Africa, where he also first became a slave at the hands of the Portuguese. He continued to be a slave when the Portuguese sold him to the Spanish in the city of Seville. At that time, he became the property of Señor Dorantes.

When the Navarez expedition arrived in what would become the United States in 1528, and since our Moroccan hero was still the slave of Señor Dorantes at that time, Estevanico became a slave on his third continent (Africa, Europe and North America).

When the Dorantes party, complete with the African slave, arrived in New Spain in early 1539, Estevanico either was sold, or his rights were transferred to the governor of New Spain, Antonio de Mendoza. When Estevanico was sent by Señor Mendoza north to search for the seven cities of gold, it was under the aegis of the Mexican governor.

Bekunuru Kubayanda (1944–1991), a scholar and native of Ghana, was educated on the same three continents, but he also wrote extensively on the idea of the tri-continental perspective in his 1990 essay entitled "On Colonial/Imperial Discourse and Contemporary Critical Theory."

Perhaps the most interesting aspect of this essay is that Kubayanda cautions against the use of neo-Marxist critical theory because it has "the potential not only to exclude, or marginalize, but also to lie about its universality." In this same essay, Mr. Kubayanda also pointed out that in the mid-twentieth century neo-Marxist revival of the 1940s and

1950s, there already were some staunch critics of the looming Critical Theory on the horizon, particularly in France.

In the mind of Mr. Kubayanda, the most important critic of Critical Theory at the time was French scholar Albert Memmi and his work, *The Colonizer and the Colonized*, originally published in France in 1957. Memmi faulted the New Left for underestimating the national aspect of colonial liberation.

Still, with this said, it is quite clear that Estevanico's tri-continental perspective had a great deal to do with his life in America from 1528 to 1539. Indeed, as far as we know, our Morrocan slave was the first man to be enslaved on three continents—Africa, Europe and North America. Of his many talents and aspects of his life, this tri-continental perspective must not be ignored in the life of Estevanico of Azemmour.

As we have suggested earlier, on the morning of his death at Hawikuh in March of 1539, if Estevanico prayed, it was not to the Judeo-Christian God. Rather, it would have been a petition to Allah, the god Muhammad, the prophet of Islam. And since he died at dawn, the prayer that he said was in classical Arabic.

In transliterated Arabic, the Fajr prayer begins this way:

Subhanna kallah huma wa bee hum deka wa ta bara kusmuka wa ta Allah jaduka wa la ilaha ghairuk.

In English, this may be rendered:

You are glorified, o Allah, and praised. Your name is blessed, your majesty is exulted. And none has the right to worship anyone but You.

A few passages later in the Fajr, we come to the words that surely Estevanico must have prayed that morning of his death. These are:

A'odohoo Billahi minash-shaytannir-rajeem.

Or:

I seek refuge in Allah from Satan, the accursed.

If Estevanico did utter this prayer and words of forgiveness and mercy were on his lips before he was murdered, then in a real way, the slave from Azemmour would have reverted back to the first of his tri-continental roots, his childhood in north Africa.

Estevanico (1500–1539). Also known as Esteban de Dorantes, Estebanico, and Esteban the Moor. Moorish slave and explorer of the American southwest.
Courtesy of Granger.

# Bibliography

**Books**

Adorno, Rolena and Patrick Charles. *The Narrative of Cabeza de Vaca*. Lincoln and London: University of Nebraska Press, 1999.

Aiton, Arthur Scott. *Antonio de Mendoza: First Viceroy of New Spain*. New York: Russell and Russell, 1927. Reprinted in 1967.

Alacron, Hernando de. *Documentos Ineditos* in *Conservapedia*. July 13, 2016.

Allen, Theodore. *RCIAL Oppression and Social Control*. New York: Verso Books, 1994.

Arrington, Carolyn. *Estevanico*. Fort Worth: Eakin Press, 1986.

Bandelier, Frances. *The Relación*. Washington, DC, 1905.

———. *Historical Documents Related to Mexico, Nueva Vizcaya and Approaches Thereto to 1773*. Philadelphia: Franklin Classics, 2018.

Bennett, Lerone. *Before the Mayflower*. Eastford: Martino Fine Books, 2016.

Brandon, William. *The Rise and Fall of North American Indians*. Lanham, Maryland: Roberts Rinehart Publishing, 2003.

Breuil, Henri. *The Men of the Stone Age*. New York: Praeger Press, 1980.

——. *The Cave at Altamira*. Madrid: *Tipogragia de Archivos*, 1935.

Cantor, Carrie Nichols. *Francisco Vásquez de Coronado: The Search for the Cities of Gold*. Mexico City: Proud Heritage, Hispanic Library, 2003.

Cisneros, Jose. *Cabezade Vaca and His Three Companions on the Texas Coast*. Kindle Editions, 2019.

Clayton, Lawrence. *The De Soto Chronicles*. Tuscaloosa: University of Alabama Press, 1995.

Covey, Cyclone. *Cabeza de Vaca's Adventures in the Unknown Interior of America*. New York: Create Space, 2016.

de Casteneda, Pedro. *The Narrative of the Expedition of Coronado*. Deep River, Connecticut: Lakeside Press, 2002. Originally published in 1896.

Delgado, Richard. *Critical Race Theory: An Introduction*. Third edition. New York: NYU Press, 2017.

de Vaca, Cabeza. *Relación: Chronicles of the Narváez Expedition*. New York: Penguin Books, 2002.

Douglas, Aaron. *Into Bondage*. New York, 1946.

Favata, Martin. *The Account of Álvar Núñez Cabeza de Vaca*. Houston: Arte Publico Press, 2001.

Flint, Richard. *No Settlement, No Conquest*. Albuquerque: University of New Mexico Press, 2018. Estevanico is discussed on pp. 27–29 and 33–35.

Frazer, James. *The Golden Bough*. New York: Collier Books, 1922. Reprinted 1985.

Garrido, Juan. *On Time, Being, and Hunger*. New York: Fordham University Press, 2012.

——. *Ser O No: Iinder Un Dialogo Con Tu Futuro Yo*. Madrid: Respendalados Libros, 2018.

Goodwin, Robert. *Crossing the Continent 1527 to 1540: The Story of the First African in American History.* New York: Harper Perennials, 2009.

Hallenbeck, Cleve. *The Journey of Fray Marcos de Niza.* Dallas: Southern Methodist University Press, 1987.

Hammond, George P. *Narratives of the Coronado Expedition, 1540–1542.* Albuquerque: University of New Mexico Press, 1940.

Hannah-Jones, Nikole. *The 1619 Project: A New Origin Story.* New York: One World Publishing, 2021.

Hemming, John. *The Conquest of the Incas.* New York: Harcourt Brace, 1970.

Herrick, Dennis. *Esteban: The African Slave Who Explored America.* Albuquerque: University of New Mexico Press, 2018.

Jabar, Kareem Abdul, and Alan Steinberg. *Black Profiles in Courage: A Legacy of African-American Achievement.* New York: Perennial Books, 2000.

Jaynes, Gerald D., ed. "Estevanico." *Encyclopedia of African American Society.* London: Sage publications, 2002.

Katz, William Loren. *The Black West.* Garden City: Doubleday and Company, 1971.

Lalami, Laila. *The Moor's Account.* New York: Vintage Books, 2014.

Maura, J. F. *Nueva Interpretaciones de Sobre las Adventuras de Alvar Nunez de Cabezade Vaca, Esteban de Dorantes, y Fray Marcos de Niza.* 2002.

Najera, Pedro de. *Narrative of the Coronado Expedition.* New York: Lakeside Publishing, 2002.

Oachs, Emily Rose. *The Cave of Altamira (Digging up the Past).* Salamanca: Spanish National Library, 2019.

Oviedo, Gonzalo Fernández. *Historia General y Natural de las Indias*. Madrid: Nuevo Mundo, 2007.

Parish, Helen Rand. *Estebanico*. Trotwood: LWF Publications, 1974.

Parry, J. H. *The Spanish Seaborne Empire*. New York: Knopf, 2012.

Pena, Enrique. *Relación de Álvar Núñez Cabeza de Vaca*. New York: Wentworth Books, 2018.

Purchas, Samuel. *Purchas: His Pilgrims*. London, 1625.

Ramusio, Giovanni. *Della navigazioni e dei viaggi.* Roma: KKIEN Publ. Int., 2015.

Remington, Frederick. *Coronado on His Quest*. New York, 1898.

Reséndez, Andrés. *The Other Slavery*. New York: Mariner Books, 2017.

Ricks, J. Brent. *Kachinas: Spirit Beings of the Hopi*. Albuquerque: Avanya Press, 1993.

Royles, Dan, ed. *The Schlager Anthology of Black America*. New York: Milestones of American History, 2022.

Samuel, Jeremie. *Do You Know Estevanico?* New York: Create Space, 2016.

Sando, Joe S. *Pueblo Nations: Eight Centuries of Pueblo Indian History*. New York: Clear light Publishers, 1992.

Sauer, Carl. *The Road to Cibola*. London: Hassell Street Press, 2021.

Shepherd, Elizabeth. *The Discoveries of Esteban the Black*. New York: Dodd Mead, 1971.

Smith, Buckingham. *The Relación*. Washington, DC, 1855.

Telushkin, Joseph. *Jewish Literacy*. New York: William Morrow, 1991.

Ternaux-Compans, Henri. *Voyages, Relations, et Memories*. Paris, 1837.

Terrell, John Upton. *Apache Chronicles*. New York World Publishing, 1972.

———. *Estevanico*. Los Angeles: Westernlore Books, 1968.

Van Sertima, Ivan. *They Came Before Columbus: The African presence in Ancient America*. New York: Random House, 1976.

Vernam, Roger. *Morning Star: A Little Pueblo Girl*. New York: Platt and Munk,1935.

Vicchio, Stephen. *Muslim Slaves in the Chesapeake 1634–1865*. Minneapolis: Wisdom Editions, 2019.

———. *Biblical Figures in the Islamic Faith*. Eugene: Wipf and Stock Publishers, 2016.

Winship, George Parker. *The Journey of Coronado*. Oxford: Palala Press, 2016.

Zronik, John Paul, ed. "Sieur de la Salle." *New World Adventurers in the Footsteps of Explorers*. Lisbon: Tapa Blanda, 2005.

## Articles

Adorno, Rolena. "Estebanico's Legacy." *Guided History*. Boston, 1997.

Allen, Anne. "Estevanico, the Moor." *American History Feature*. August 1997. Later republished February 1, 2017, *History Net*, https://bit.ly/3UhUFmQ.

Anonymous. "de Niza Expedition." *Associated Press*. July 12, 2017.

———. "The 1539 Marcos de Niza Expedition." *Planetary Science*. November 15, 2010.

———. "The Jewish Community in Azemmour." *World Jewish Congress*. March 15, 2020.

———. "The Zuni: A Mysterious People." Zuni pueblo of New Mexico, 1997.

Bloom, Lansing. "Fray Marcos de Niza and His Journey to Cibola." *New Mexico Historical Review* 3, no 4 (1947): 415–486.

Bogen, David S. "Mathias de Sousa: Maryland's First Colonist of African Descent." *Maryland Historical Society Magazine* 96, no. 1 (2001): 68–85.

Cassidy, Vincent H. deP. "Columbus and the Negro." *The Phylon Quarterly* 20, no. 3 (October 1959).

Conant, Elizabeth. "Historical Interpreter Profile: Estevanico." https://bit.ly/3jkGIb0.

Contreras, Russell. "Mystery Confines Estebanico, Black Explorer of US Southwest." *Associated Press*. February 26, 2018. https://bit.ly/3BWtQOD.

Corcos, D. "Rabbi Joseph Adibe." *Sefunot* 10 (1966).

DeGratia, Ted. "Cabeza de Vaca." A TV series on the Moroccan hero. It is also a series of images in Andrés Reséndez's *A Land so Strange: The Epic Journey of Cabeza de Vaca*. New York: Basic Books, 2007.

Garrido, Juan. "Probenza." *Black History*. 2009.

Gordon, Richard A. "Following Estevanico: The Influential Presence of an African Slave in Sixteenth Century New World Historiography." *Colonial Latin-American Review* 15, no. 2 (December 2006).

Haselby, Sam. "Muslims of Early America." *Aeon*. May 20, 2019.

Hicham, Mohamed de. "Tariq Ibn Zayad." Kindle Editions. 2011.

Heure, Derniere. "Culture: The Saints of Azemmour." *Le Matin*. May 3, 2003.

George Kittridge. "Some Lost Works of Cotton Mather." Oxford: Palala Press, 2015.

Gordon, Jonathan. 'Ten Greatest Explorers in History." *Biography*. August 30, 2020.

Gordon-Reed, Annette. "Black America's Neglected Origin Stories." *Atlantic*. June 2021.

Ilahiane, Hsain. "Estevan De Dorantes, the Moor or the Slave?" *The Journal of North African Studies* 5, no. 3 (2000).

Kelly, McKenna. "Exploring Estevanico." *Tampa Magazine*. May 25, 2018. This article contains a photograph of John Houser's bust of Estevanico.

Kelton, Sarah. "The Story of Estevanico." Published in *Beatport*. Ms. Kelton, however, makes a number of mistakes about Estevanico's biography including her claim that he was born in 1490.

Koo, Kathryn. "Strangers in the House of God: Cotton Mather, Onesimus, and an experiment in Christian slaveholding." *American Antiquarian* (2007): 143–175.

Kubayanda, Joseph. "On Colonial-Imperial Discourse and Contemporary Critical Theory." *Despositio*. 14, no. 36–38, pp. 25–37.

Laskier, Michael. "The instability of Moroccan Jewry and the Moroccan Press in the First Decade After Independence." *Jewish History* 1, no.1 (1986).

Lekson, Stephen. "Kivas." *The Architecture of Chico Canyon, New Mexico*. Salt Lake City: University of Utah Press, 2007.

——. "The Idea of the Kiva in Anasazi Archeology." *Kiva* 53 (Spring 1988).

Logan, Rayford. "Estevanico." *Phylon* 1, no. 4 (1940).

McCrae, Bernie. "Estevanico." www.thehistortnet.com.america.

McDonald, Dedra. "Intimacy and Empire: Indian-African Interaction in Spanish Colonial New Mexico." *American Indian Quarterly* 22, nos. 1 and 2 (1998): pp. 134–156.

McKenny, Kelly. "Exploring Estevanico." *South Tampa Bay Magazine*. May 25, 2018.

Moore, R. Edward. "The Karankawa Indians." texasindians.com/karank.htm.

Morse, Kim. "Esteban of Azemmour and His New World Adventures." *Aramco World*. March–April 2002.

Núñez, Gabriel Gonzales. "Trans-Politics in a Linguistically Diverse World." *Journal of Ethno-Politics and Minority Issues in Europe* 15, no. 1 (2016): pp. 1–18.

Richmond, Dr. Douglas. "The Emergence of Afro-Tejano Society During the Spanish Colonial Period in Texas, 1528–1700." Prairie View A&M University. https://bit.ly/3jRchcP. Dr. Richmond makes several observations about Estevanico. He chose the 1528 date because of the arrival of Estevanico to Texas.

Schkloven, Emma. "Looking Deeper at the Massive New Juneteenth Mural in Galveston." *Houstonia*. June 18, 2021. https://bit.ly/3WSfHe4.

Selin, Shannon. "The Karankawa Indians of Texas." *Imagining the Bounds of History*. January 2017.

Simour, Lhoussain. "(De)slaving history: Mostafa al-Azemmouri, the sixteenth-century Moroccan captive in the tale of conquest." *European Review of History* 20, no 3 (2013). https://bit.ly/40g11aE.

Smith, Meg. "African-American Men." *The Washington Post*. January 7, 2005.

Terrell, John Upton. "Estevanico." *Desert Magazine* 33, no. 7 (1970).

Torres-Spelliscy, Ciara. "Everyone is Talking About 1619 But that is Not Actually When Slavery in America Started." *Washington Post*. August 23, 2019.

Valley-Fox, Anne. "Estevan, the Moor." In *El Palacio*. Winter 2014.

Wagner, Henry. "The de Niza Exploration to Cibola." *New Mexico Historical Review* 3, no. 4 (1932).

## Internet Sources

"African Americans at Jamestown." Historic Jamestowne. https://bit.ly/3Z7tpLg.

"Black Explorers We Should Celebrate Instead of Columbus." The Grio, https://on.thegrio.com/3ImYMf4.

Chandler, D. L. "Little known Black History Fact." Blackamericaweb.com. https://bit.ly/3ueVfXN.

Encyclopedia.com. "Estevanico." https://bit.ly/3ETqjkX.

"Estevanico: North American Explorer." Famous Explorers, https://bit.ly/3jKZc4E.

Hutchins, Rachel. "Non-Muslim Integration into the Early Caliphate Through the Use of Surrender Agreements." University of Arkansas, History Undergraduate Honors Theses. https://bit.ly/3i9GGCs.

Johnson, John G. "Pánfilo de Narváez." https://bit.ly/3GdLChG.

Professor A. L. I. "Estevanico," sfbayview.com. May 20, 2011, https://bit.ly/3Qctw4w.

Enriching Medicine Through Diversity. https://bit.ly/3X7P6sO.

Theodore Allen on Tom Pope Show. WSMX Radio, September 8, 2000. Allen's view can be seen in his *Summary of the Argument of the Invention of the White Race*, https://bit.ly/3WSk-WcC.

American Negro Exposition in Chicago [1940.] featured Diorama honoring Estevanico.

"Esteban: Slave, conquistador, and the first African in Texas," tbhpp.org/estevanico.html.

Black historyheroes, https://bit.ly/3J8Zj4z.

Flint, Richard and Shirley Cushing Flint. Esteban the Moor, https://bit.ly/3WF3Vnb.

Chipman, Donald E. "Estevanico." https://bit.ly/3Z4kZEJ.

"Estevanico." *Wikipedia*. February 1, 2017. en.wikipedia.org/wiki/Estevanico.

Otterness, Anders. "Cabeza de Vaca and Estevanico." https://bit.ly/3WXkRWd.

   Legends of America. "Andres Dorantes de Carranza – Spanish Explorer." Kathy Alexander. Updated October 2022. https://bit.ly/3B0xA1i.

Shamsie, Muneeza. "Reconstructing the story of Mustapha/Estebanico: A Moor in the New World: An interview with Laila Lalami." *Journal of Post-Colonial Writing* 52, no 2 (2016): 195–200, https://bit.ly/3IkfOdV.

The National Park Service now maintains the San José de Gracia mission church in New Mexico and is on the NPS's Historic American Buildings Survey, https://bit.ly/3Gd3I3p.

The Social Studies Superstore has developed a middle school education unit on Estevanico. It is called, "Middle School-Estevanico: An Early African Explorer of the New World." https://bit.ly/3Ggh3It.

Turner, Steve. "The Racial Frontier Rare Photographs of Blacks Who Forged Lives in the Old West." *Truewestmagazine.com* has a collection of images it calls "Estevanico," in their collection, https://bit.ly/3Z4QBKi.

"The Dates and Events of Estevanico's Life," https://bit.ly/3H1oAex.

**Maps**

Cabexa de Vaca's route. https://bit.ly/3UoRBFq.

"Estevanico." Map posted by Carter Nelson, October 30, 2015. https://bit.ly/3OS6ora.

"Estevanico – Biography." enchantedlearning.com. https://bit.ly/3iyn3Eg.

"The Mysterious Journey of Friar Marcos de Niza." Planetary Scient Institute. Map of Estevanico's 1539 trek from Mexico City to Cibola. https://bit.ly/3B0GMTs.

"Estevanico." Map of Estevanico's travels 1527 to 1539. https://bit.ly/3ETCaPZ.

Two maps on the inside front and back covers of J. U. Terrel's *Estevanico the Black* depict his travel from Florida to Mexico and Mexico City to Cibola in Northwest New Mexico and the place of his death at the hands of the Zuni Indians.

## Art Sources

"All the World is Human." PBS film. 2002.

Álvar Cabeza de Vaca bust. Museum de Puerto Iguazo, Argentina.

"Álvar Núñez Cabeza de Vaca." *Encyclopedia Britannica*. Includes a copy of a print of the Spanish explorer Estevanico and several Indian guides who accompanied the party to New Mexico from Mexico City in 1539.

Amy Lowe. "Estebanico, The Black: A Story Rarely Told." 2021.

Anonymous. "Estevanico." *Granger Historical Pictures Archive*.

Band Erased from Time. "The Ballad of Estevanico." 2017.

Borunda, Daniel. "John Houser, sculptor of El Paso's Twelve Travelers Statues, Dies at 82." *El Paso Times*. January 11, 2018. https://bit.ly/3X83e5k.

Byrd, Donald. "Estevanico." On *Electric Byrd* album. 1970.

*Cabeza de Vaca*. 1991 film directed by Nicolás Echevarría, starring Juan Diego and Roberto Sosa. It tells the tale of the shipwreck, the building of the five rafts and the coming to Texas.

"Cabeza de Vaca, Estevanico, and the Other Survivors." *San Anto-nio Report*. https://bit.ly/3vCN0Wl. Includes a painting of Estevanico and the other survivors. Cabeza de Vaca is in the center, Estevanico on his immediate left, and another White Spaniard in front of him. Behind de Vaca is the fourth survivor who sits on his hunches. The four survivors gaze at the valley below and the mountains in the distance.

*Cortes With the Moorish Soldier Estevanico Entering Mexico*. https://amzn.to/44DTJjg.

Dallas Historical Society has a collection of materials related to Cabeza de Vaca and Estevanico, including the following items:

1. A beaded leather bag containing flint arrowheads like those used by the Zuni warriors who killed Estevanico.
2. A gourd rattle with owl feathers and assorted pieces of turquoise beads similar to the medicine men gourds used by the Moroccan slave and his comrades.
3. The copy of a receipt given to Andrés Dorantes de Carranza pertaining to the ownership of "one Moroccan-born slave to Viceroy Antonio de Mendoza." The fee for the transfer of property was twelve silver pesados.
4. A signed copy of Cabeza de Vaca's *Relación* was given to the king of Spain in 1537 and published in Zamora, Spain, in 1521.

Datus, Jay, painted a Spanish-era mural for the Arizona State Library in 1937 and 1939. It commemorated the Spanish missionaries and conquistadors coming to Arizona. Two of the figures in the mural are to the far right of the painting. One is Fray Marcos de Niza, and the other to his left is Estevan the Moor. The Black man is much taller than the monk. The slave is clean-shaven and wears a North-African headdress. There are about a dozen figures in the mural, one conquistador in battle dress; four Franciscans, including Fray de Niza; five Native Americans; and the Black man, Estevanico.

*Estevanico*. 2016 film starring British actor Idriss Elba, who plays the title character whose name is *Mustapha Zemmouri*.

Flint, Richard. *No Settlement, No Conquest: A History of the Corona-do Entrada*. University of New Mexico Press, 2018. Contains an illustration of Estevanico by graphic artist Jose Cisneros.

Fox, Joe. "Estevanico," painting/poster.

Gomez, Adrian, editor of the "Arts and Entertainment" section of the *Albuquerque Journal* (February 19, 2022), wrote an article entitled, "Children's Radio Show Goes On-Line to Deliver Southwest History." Katie Stone, the subject of the article, instituted a radio show called the "Children's Hour" that began around the year 2000. Among the programs developed by Ms. Stone is one on Estevanico.

Hayes, Merdies. "Estevanico: The Man, the Myth, the Legend." *Our Weekly*. February 15, 2019. https://bit.ly/3WOZeau. Ms. Hayes gives a good summary of what we know of the life of the Moroccan slave. The cover of the periodical also features a painting of Estevanico. In the image, our hero has bushy hair and a full beard and is dressed in a white smock/shirt.

*Historica: The National Treasures Book of Secrets*. A cartoon version of the life of Estevanico. He is dressed in a tattered white tunic and dark shorts. He has a bag hanging from his shoulder across his chest, and his hands rest on a wooden stick about three feet in length.

Kelley, McKenna. "Exploring Estevanico." *Tampa Magazine*. May 25, 2018.

Kouko Kaga is a mural of Estebanico Azemur that still exists on a wall in Azemmour, Morocco.

L'Heureux, Marianne. *Estevanico 1539*, painting.

Lalami, Laila. "Estebanico in the Visual Arts." https://bit.ly/3ieA5a4. The essay contains four images of the Moroccan hero. August 5, 2014.

Mariner's Museum, Newport News, Virginia, in 2021, sought to identify twenty-one previously unidentified African American men
from an archived photograph depicting men who worked on
the construction of the museum. In regard to that same project,
the museum also revealed that it has a collection of early African American images, including some of Estevanico.

Mass Effect. "MSV Estevanico." Video game 020.

Paradox Interactive Europa Universalis. Video gamer. 2015.

Rainwater, Liv, a Native American poet, completed a Haiku poem
on Estevanico in which she gives a sense of the struggles of
Estevanico. Ms. Rainwater is from North Carolina.

Sam Patrick. "Estevanico." Miriam Matthews Photograph Collection
at the UCLA Library. 1969.

Tayler, Luis. "Estevanico," painting. 2020.

The *de Niza* Stone. South Mountain, Arizona. Discovered in 1922.

"The Mysterious Cities of Gold." An anime series with a character
named Esteban, which appears to be loosely based on the story
of Estevanico.

Tyranno Nija. "Estevanico: Moorish Explorer." *Deviant Art*. 2002.

*Uncharted: The Golden Abyss*. 2011 video game developed by Sony
Computer Entertainment. The game was originally released in
Japan in 2011 and worldwide in 2012. "Esteban is a character
in the game. In one episode, he is shown dead, sitting on the
"Throne of Gold."

Valley-Fox, Anne, an American poet, completed a poem entitled
"Estevan the Moor" and published it in the journal *El Palacio*
in 2009. The poem also appears in her collection called *How
Shadows are Bundled*, published by the University of New
Mexico Press, also in 2009. Ms. Valley-Fox ends her poem
with the following words:

Surrounding his ebony skin hissing resilience, the Moor

Strode North towards riches and women.

O! the bolt from out of the blue

As Zuni arrows pierced his clamorous heart.

Yang, Jeffrey. "Estevanico." *Poetry*. July–August 2017.

## Music Sources

Bouraque, Tarek. *Time Machine Research and Approach* (2020). CUNY Academic Works. https://bit.ly/3Ggke2O.

East Coast Hip Hop released an album entitled *Two Nights in Marrakesh*, December 2021. One of the songs on the album is entitled "Esteban, the Moor."

Estevanico (performer). "Whole Moroccan Songs."

Estevanico International Festival, on April 20 and 21, 2022, took place at the Plaza de la Luna in Pensacola, Florida. African-American writer Robin Reshard wrote "An Insider's Look at Black History Month in Pensacola" in *Pensacola Magazine*, giving a good description of "Esteban, the Moor" and some of the music planned for the festival.

Fabre-Carter, Leo, Frederic Calmes, and Arthur Narcy, performed a two-hour concert on Sunday, December 13, 2020, at the Dar Batha in Fez, Morocco. The concert was dedicated to the life of Estevanico.

Jones, Estevanico, an American musician and singer who mentions his namesake in many of his songs.

Morassi, Bruno, an Italian composer, wrote a piece of music entitled "Fray Marcos and Estevanico" in 2018.

Obermann Working Group, made up of a dozen musicians, gathered in the basement of an Iowa City home to record their composition entitled "Esteban and the Children of the Sun" in mid-June of 2021. The group had been brought together in 2018 to discuss the possibility of creating a musical suite based on Cabeza de Vaca's narrative. The piece was later performed at the Obermann Center for Advanced Studies on Church Street in Iowa City.

Tats Cru. *Estevanico*. Bronx, New York, 2010.

Toro, Guillermo del, director and composer, has listed Laila Lalami's *The Moor's Account* as one of the sources for his books, television, films and music.

US Government honored the memory of Estevanico as "The First Moroccan to Explore America," at least according to a February 11, 2021, report from the *Morocco World News*.

## Government Sources

Land Office Record MSA A 5920. Sections 1, 19, 20 and 37.

Maryland General Assembly Record, 1637–1658. MSA S-977-1.

Land Grant Record MSA 5920-4.

Ceremony to honor Zipporah Potter Adkins. Mayor of Boston, Massachusetts. May 20, 2014.

*Estevanico: Black Explorer in Spanish Texas*. Texas Legislative Reference Library, Austin, Texas.

The Federal poverty level in the United States can be found at https://bit.ly/2S4PeYw. In 2021, it stands at $12,880 for individuals and up to $44,660 for a family of eight.

We have also consulted various bestowals of land grants in what became the United States both by the Crown of Spain and Government of the United States of America, from the sixteenth to the nineteenth centuries.

Among the sources we have consulted for Spanish and American Land Grants are:

Alonzo, Armando C. "Mexican-American Land Grant Adjudication." https://bit.ly/3jS7yr3.

Simmonds, Ricardo. "Mexican Land Grants in Colorado," in *Colorado Encyclopedia*. April 18, 2021.

Van Ness, John R. and Christine M., editors. *Spanish and Mexican Land Grants in New Mexico and Colorado*. Manhattan, Kansas: Sunflower University Press, 1980.

Castillo, Richard Griswold del. *The Treaty of Guadalupe Hidalgo: A Legacy of Conflict*. Norman: University of Oklahoma Press, 1990.

*Guide to Spanish and Mexican Land Grants in South Texas*. Austin, Texas General Land Office, 1988.

Garcia, Richard D. and Todd Howland. "Determining the Legitimacy of Spanish Land Grants in Colorado: Conflicting Values, Legal Pluralism and Demystification of the Sangre de Cristo/Rael Case." In *Chicana/o Law Review* 16, no. 1 (1995).

Hafen, Leroy R. "Mexican Land Grants in Colorado." *Colorado Magazine* 4, no. 3 (May 1927).

Kosek, Jake. *Understories: The Political Life of Forests in Northern New Mexico*. Durham: Duke University Press, 2006.

Simmons, Virginia McConnell. *The San Luis Valley: Land of the Six-Armed Cross*. 2nd edition. Niwot: University Press of Colorado, 1999.

All of the sources listed above make many references to the bestowal of Land Grants by Spain, Mexico, and the United States. There are also extant many Spanish and Portuguese government sources during the Age of Exploration. We have incorporated many of these sources in this study.

# Endnotes

1    Little else is known of De Soto's slave "Robles." He is mentioned in Dolly Chisholm and Thomas D. Hills, "Hernando De Soto and the Impact of Spanish Exploration in Georgia," Georgia Historical Society, https://bit.ly/3xD1PJe.

2    Ciara Torres-Spelliscy, "Everyone is Talking About 1619. But That is Not Actually When Slavery in America Started," *The Washington Post*, August 23, 2019. Johan Biscayan is also mentioned in Robert Keith Collins' review of "African Creeks: Estelvste and the Creek Nation," *Journal of Southern History* 75, no. 3 (August 2009), 774–775.

3    Clayton, 21.

4    Juan Garrido, "Probanza," discussed in "Juan Garrido, Hernán Cortés and Mexico City," published in *Black History*, as well as in the article entitled "Juan Garrido" in *Imagining la Florida* in 2009.

5    For more on "Antonio" or Anthony Johnson, see Stephen J. Vicchio, *Muslim Slaves in the Chesapeake: 1634 to 1865* (Minneapolis: Wisdom Editions, 2019), 45–55.

6    Peter Martyr (1457–1526) was chaplain to the court of King Ferdinand II of Aragon and Queen Isabella I of Castile. He also chronicled Spanish explorations in the New World.

7    Vincent Cassidy, "Columbus and the Negro," *The Phylon Quarterly* 20, no. 3 (1959), 294–297.

8    Ibid., 295–296.

9    Theodore W. Allen, *Racial Oppression and Social Control* (New York: Verso Books, 1994), 43.

10    For more on Altamira, Spain, and Lascaux, France, and their cave drawings, see Emily Rose Oachs, *The Cave of Altamira: Digging up the Past* (Salamanca: Encuadernacion de Biblioteca, 2019). This text is only twenty-four pages but was very helpful in our research.

11    Henri Breuil (1877–1961) was ordained a priest in 1900 and was introduced

to Paleolithic studies by Emile Cartailhac in October of 1902 when he opened the Altamira Cave in Spain.

12    See, for example, *The Men of the Stone Age* (New York: Praeger Press, reprinted in 1980); and *The Cave at Altamira* (*Tipographia de Archivos*, 1935). These contain examples of Sympathetic Magic in Henri Breuil's works.

13    This identity question in regard to Estevanico is taken up by Raymond W. Logan in his 1940 article in *Phylon*, simply called "Estevanico."

14    "African Americans at Jamestown," National Park Service, retrieved 2/5/21, https://bit.ly/3mgcLXU.

15    Martin A. Favata, trans., *The Account: Álvar Núñez Cabeza de Vaca's Relación* (Houston: Arte Publico Press, 2001).

16    Juan Garrido (1487–1550) was an African conquistador born in the Kingdom of the Kongo. He joined a Spanish expedition and arrived in Santo Domingo (Hispaniola) about 1502. He participated in the invasions of Puerto Rico and Cuba and also participated in Cortés's exploration of Mexico in 1519. For more on Juan Garrido, see *On Time, Being, and Hunger* (New York: Fordham University Press, 2012), 10–12.

17    Ibid., 137–138.

18    Anonymous, *History of Florida* (Miami: Captivated History, 2022), 7–17.

19    The Virginia Court decision on John Punch was made on July 9, 1640. It describes six runaway servants and a Black man who were all captured. The court sentenced them to varying degrees of punishment, with Punch's being the most severe. Punch was also declared "a slave for life" by the court.

20    Albert James Pickett, *Alabama and Incidentally Georgia and Mississippi* (Charleston: Walker and James, 1851, reprinted 2018), 1–3.

21    Anthony Johnson (?–1670) was most likely born in Angola and came to Virginia in 1622, where he became a slave owner in the Commonwealth, as well as in Maryland. His court case was decided on March 8, 1655, when the Northampton County Court ruled in his favor and declared that he was "a free man." For more Anthony Johnson, aka, Antonio, see Stephen J. Vicchio, *Muslim Slaves in the Chesapeake: 1634 to 1865* (Minneapolis: Wisdom Editions, 2019), 12–14.

22    Pedro Alonso Nino (1468–1505) was a Spanish explorer known as "El Negro." He was born in Moguer, Spain, and is said to have participated in the first and third of Columbus' voyages to the New World. For more on Nino, see Vincent H. deP. Cassidy, "Columbus and 'The Negro,'" *The Phylon Quarterly*, 20, no. 3 (October 1959).

23 Monument at Saint Francisco Convent, Moguer, Spain. Nino also had two brothers, Juan and Francisco, both of whom served on the *Nina* in 1492.

24 Cassidy, 1.

25 Andrés Reséndez, *The Other Slavery: The Uncovered Story of Indian Enslavement in America* (New York: Houghton Mifflin Harcourt, 2016).

26 Tariq Ibn Ziyad (670–720), also known simply as Tarik in English, was a Berber Umayyad commander who initiated the Muslim Umayyad conquest of the Visigothic Hispania (present-day Spain and Portugal) from 711 to 718. He had a large army and approached the peninsula from the Strait of Gibraltar on the North African coast.

27 Mohamed de Hicham, *Tariq ibn Ziyad: Life of a Legend* (Kindle Edition, 2021), 14–17.

28 Ibid., 40–42.

29 Abd ar-Rahman was the founder of the Emirate of Cordoba. He was instrumental in bringing Islamic rule to Spain.

30 In 800 CE, Pope Leo III crowned Charlemagne the Emperor of Rome. The year before, in 799, the pope was abused by Roman soldiers who tried to gouge out his eyes and pull out his tongue, so Leo escaped and fled to Charlemagne.

31 For more on the decline of the Umayyads, see Rachel Hutchings' 2020 Honors Thesis entitled, "Non-Muslim Integration into the Early Caliphate Through the Use of Surrender Agreements," *History Undergraduate Honors Theses*, https://bit.ly/3n58UNy.

32 For more on the Jewish community in Azemmour, see "Moroccan Jewish Community Representative Sits Down for Exclusive Interview," *World Jewish Congress*, March 6, 2020, https://bit.ly/3N80QGH.

33 Rabbi Joseph Adibe was the head of the Jewish community in Azemmour, which consisted of 2,500 Jews in the early sixteenth century around the time of the birth of Estevanico. See D. Corcos, *Sefunot* 10 (1966): 63–69; and A Baiao, *Inquisicao em Portugal* (1921), 128ff.

34 David Ha Reuveni (died 1532) is also known as "David Reubeni." He was a Jewish adventurer with grandiose plans inspired by the mystical visions of Solomon Molcho.

35 Michael M. Laskier, "The Instability of Moroccan Jewry and the Moroccan Press in the First Decade After Independence," *Jewish History* 1, no. 1 (1986).

36 For more on the Edict of Expulsion, see Joseph Telushkin, *Jewish Literacy* (New York: William Morrow and Co., 1991). Also: "Spain's Window for

Sephardic Jews to Seek Nationality Closes," *Associated Press*, October 1, 2019.

37    Laskier, 17–18.

38    *Azama* was originally an ancient Phoenician word that meant "olive." It was also the name of an ancient city occupied by the Phoenicians before it fell under the influences of Carthage and the Romans. Under the latter, Azama experienced a period of great prosperity.

39    In 1513, Governor Moulay Zayam refused to pay the tribute and the Spanish sent a massive fleet of five hundred ships and fifteen thousand soldiers.

40    Ferdinand Magellan is said to have sustained a serious leg injury at the Battle of Azemmour.

41    The latest population figures for 2022 in Azemmour is 41,128 residents.

42    The *Dar El Baroud* was also traditionally a bathhouse in Tangier with directions inside the doorway stating that there were separate sections for men and women, as is suggested in *Al-Qur'an's Al-Ahzab, ayat,* or verse 53.

43    Derniere Heure, "Culture: Les Saints d'Azemmour," *Le Matin*, May 3, 2003.

44    As we shall see later in this study, scholars disagree about whether Estevanico was born in 1500 or 1503, but all agree it was in the city of Azemmour.

45    Helen Rand Parish, *Estebanico* (New York: Viking Press, 1974), 11.

46    Ibid.

47    Ibid., 11–12.

48    Ibid., 12.

49    It is possible, as well, that Estevanico was not baptized until 1522, when he first became the slave of Senior Dorantes.

50    It is not clear if Estevanico was bought by Viceroy Mendoza or borrowed.

51    For more on Antonio Mendoza, see *Literatura Comparada e Intertextualidad* (Salamanca: Arco Libros, 1994).

52    Ibid.

53    Arthur Scott Aiton, *Antonio de Mendoza: First Viceroy of New Spain* (New York: Russell and Russell, 1927, reprinted 1967).

54    J. H. Parry, *The Spanish Seaborne Empire* (New York: Knopf, 2012). John Hemming, *The Conquest of the Incas* (New York: Harcourt Brace, 1970).

55    Favata, 14.

56    Ibid.

57    For more on the Karankawa Tribe, see R. Edward Moore, "The Karankawa Indians," https://bit.ly/3y2Cfi7.

58    Favata, 20–21.

59    Ibid., 21.

60  Ibid., 22.
61  Ibid., 23–24.
62  Ibid., 24.
63  This document is owned by the Dallas Historical Society at 3939 Grand Avenue, Dallas, Texas. Other items in the same collection are the following: a beaded leather bag containing flint arrowheads and pottery remains, decorative shells, a Gourd rattle with owl feathers, and assorted turquoise beads. Presumably, these additional artifacts are like those employed by Estevanico and his comrades in their role as medicine men.
64  Favata, 24.
65  See Note 33.
66  Favata, 25–26.
67  Ibid., 26.
68  Ibid.
69  Ibid., 27–28.
70  Sir James Frazer, *The Golden Bough* (New York: Collier Books, originally published in 1922, reprinted 1985).
71  Ibid., chapter three on "Sympathetic Magic."
72  Sieur de la Salle, *New World Adventurer in the Footsteps of Explorers,* ed. John Paul Zronik (Lisbon: Tapa Blanda, 2005), 97.
73  Favata, 21.
74  Ibid.
75  Ibid., 22–23.
76  Ibid., 23.
77  For more on the "Great Kivas," see "Kivas," *Colorado Encyclopedia*; Stephen H. Lekson, *The Architecture of Chico Canyon, New Mexico* (Salt Lake City: University of Utah Press, 2007); and Stephen H. Lekson, "The Idea of the Kiva in Anasazi Archeology," *Kiva* 53 (Spring, 1988).
78  Manifest of Pánfilo de Narváez's ships mentioned in John G. Johnson's "Pánfilo de Narváez," https://bit.ly/3O1SDoB.
79  For more on the "1619 Project," see Nikole Hannah-Jones, *The 1619 Project: A New Origin Story* (New York: One World Publishing, 2021).
80  Stephen J. Vicchio, *Muslim Slaves in the Chesapeake: 1634 to 1865* (Minneapolis: Wisdom Editions, 2019), 45–51.
81  For more on Hernando de Soto, see Lawrence A. Clayton, *The De Soto Chronicles: The Expedition of Hernando de Soto to North America, 1539–1543*, two volumes (Tuscaloosa: University of Alabama Press, 1995).
82  Ibid., vol. 1, 29–34.

83   Sebastian Cabot (1482–1557) was born in Italy but made voyages for the British Crown in 1508 and 1509, where he discovered the entrance to Hudson Bay.

84   Jacques Cartier (1491–1557) is usually credited with giving the name "Canada" to the North American nation.

85   For more on these Moroccan dynasties, see Maya Shatzmiller, *From Berber State to Moroccan Empire* (Princeton: Markus Weiner Publishers, 2019).

86   For more on these fundamental beliefs in Islam, see Stephen Vicchio, *Biblical Figures in the Islamic Faith* (Eugene: Wipf and Stock Publishers, 2016), chapter one.

87   Ibn Masud, "History of Islam in the Americas," *Sunnah Muakada*, February 4, 2013, https://bit.ly/42rufEz.

88   "Moor," *Encyclopedia Britannica* (London, 1911).

89   Acts of the Apostles 8:27. Author's translation.

90   Dana Reynolds Marniche, "African History Time for the Children," Murakush Society, March 10, 2019, https://bit.ly/3zQcSRZ.

91   Isidore of Seville (560–636) was a doctor of the church and Latin father. He wrote a twenty-volume work called the *Etymologiae*.

92   Don Jaide, "The Moors of Lashbuna," *Rasta livewire*, October 18, 2012.

93   Suzanna Clarke, *A House in Fez: Building a Life in the Ancient Heart of Morocco* (New York: Pocket Books, 2008), 23–25.

94   Ibid., 25.

95   Ibid.

96   Ibid., 26–27.

97   Ibid., 27.

98   Ibid., 30.

99   King Mohammed V (1909–1961) became the king of Morocco in 1957. He only ruled until 1961.

100  King Hassan II of Morocco (1929–1999) succeeded his father, Mohammed V. He was born in Rabat and studied at the University of Bordeaux in France.

101  The Wattasid Empire in Morocco lasted from 1472 until 1554 and controlled the northern part of Morocco and ruled from its capital, Fez.

102  The Battle of Azemmour was fought on August 28 and 29, 1513. It was around that same time when Estevanico was sold into slavery or captured for that purpose by the Portuguese.

103  Clarke, 59–63.

104  Ibid., 67.

105  The Arabic word *mellah* is used when designating the Jewish quarter in a

Moroccan town or city. The word comes from the nineteenth-century noun *mallah*, which literally means "the salt area."

106    The Zaouia of Telouet contains some of the oldest Jewish families in Morocco.

107    The word *maghrib* in Classical Arabic means the "Western hinterlands."

108    Records indicate that Estevanico became the slave of Andrés Dorantes de Caranza in 1522. Five years later, they both came together to the New World.

109    Latifa Babas, "Estebanico Zemmouri: The First Moroccan to Reach the American Soil," March 7, 2017, https://bit.ly/3HEebFu.

110    The second edition of the *Relación* was published in Valladolid, Spain, in 1555. See the "Note on Primary Sources" after these Notes on the text.

111    The charges against Cabeza de Vaca were in relation to his expedition to Rio de la Plata, where male Spaniards had children with Native American women, and de Vaca did not handle the situation well.

112    Gonzalo Oviedo, *Historia General y Natural de las Indias* (Madrid: Editorial Nuevo Mundo, 2007). This text is only 104 pages, but it gives a very good summary.

113    Favata, 23–26.

114    Ibid., 26.

115    Ibid., 30.

116    Ibid.

117    Ibid., 33–34.

118    Ibid., 34.

119    Ibid.

120    Ibid.

121    Ibid., 35–36.

122    Ibid., 36.

123    Ibid., 40.

124    Ibid.

125    Ibid., 42.

126    Ibid., 45.

127    Ibid.

128    Ibid.

129    Favata, 50.

130    Most of the comments on the Zuni People come from an anonymous article entitled "The Zuni: A Mysterious People," in *Legends of America* produced by the Zuni Pueblo in New Mexico, https://bit.ly/2Pk61tR.

131    Ibid.

132  Ibid.

133  Ibid.

134  Ibid.

135  Ibid.

136  Ibid.

137  Ibid.

138  "The Zuni: A Mysterious People."

139  Favata, 52.

140  "Surviving Columbus: The Story of Pueblo People," documentary, https://bit.
     ly/3tNVcTi.

141  For more on John Houser, see Kim Morse, "Esteban of Azemmour and His
     New World Adventures," *Aramco World*, March–April 2002, 1–6.

142  Ibid., 5–6.

143  Coronado's letter to Viceroy Mendoza, December 10, 1537.

144  The Franciscans took the vows of poverty, chastity and obedience.

145  Favata, 61.

146  Ibid.

147  Ibid., 62.

148  Ibid., 64.

149  Ibid.

150  Mendoza letter, quoted in Favata, 65.

151  Cortés, quoted in Favata, 65.

152  John Upton Terrell, *Estevanico: The Black* (Los Angeles: Westernlore Press,
     1968), 43.

153  Castenada, quoted in Terrell, 44.

154  Coronado letter, December 10, 1537.

155  Ibid.

156  Rayford W. Logan, "Estevanico, Negro Discoverer of the Southwest," *Phylon*
     1 (1940), 305–314, 305.

157  Ibid.

158  *Pecos* is both the name of a city in Texas and a river that originates in north-
     central New Mexico and flows down to Texas.

159  Favata, 68.

160  Logan.

161  Ibid.

162  Anonymous, "The Fourth Voyage of Christopher Columbus (1502)," Athena
     Review 2, no. 1, 1–2.

163  The Semitic root MLK is another illustrative example. It is the basis for

Semitic words related to angels, like *Malak*, in Hebrew and *Mala'ika*, the Arabic plural. It is also the word for "king," *Melek* and *Malach* in Hebrew and Syriac.

164    Álvar Núñez Cabeza de Vaca, *Relación De Álvar Núñez Cabeza De Vaca*, ed. Enrique Pena (New York: Wentworth Press, 2018).

165    The Coahuiltecan Tribe were among the Native Americans who inhabited the Rio Grande River Valley in what is now South Texas and Northeastern Mexico. The various tribes were hunter-gatherers first encountered by Europeans in the sixteenth century.

166    Favata, 74–75.

167    Ibid., 75.

168    Ibid., 76.

169    *Relación De Álvar Núñez Cabeza De Vaca.*

170    Ibid. In classical Castilian Spanish, the word "Maliacones," means "bad words" or "bad speech," and thus sometimes used in the sixteenth century by the Spanish gentlemen class to be a synonym for "curses."

171    The Karankawa Tribe was a group of Native Americans encountered by the survivors of the Narváez expedition. For more on this group, see Shannon Selin, "The Karankawa Indians of Texas," *Imagining the Bounds of History*, January 2017, https://bit.ly/3ycWwBD.

172    Favata, 80.

173    Ibid.

174    Gabriel Gonzales Núñez, "Translation Policy in a Linguistically Diverse World," *Journal of Ethnopolitics and Minority Issues in Europe* 15, no. 1 (2016), 1–18.

175    Ibid., 1–2.

176    Ibid., 2.

177    Senior Dorantes bought Estevanico at a slave auction in Spain in 1522.

178    Laila Lalami, *The Moor's Account* (New York: Vintage Books, 2014).

179    Ibid., 53–54.

180    Ibid., Introduction.

181    Favata., 81.

182    Jeffrey Yang, "Estevanico," Poetry Foundation, July–August 2017, https://bit.ly/3tVPNcT.

183    John Upton Terrell, *Estevanico: The Black* (Los Angeles: Westernlore Press, 1968).

184    John Upton Terrill, "Estevanico," *Desert Magazine* 33, no. 7 (1970).

185    John Upton Terrill, *Apache Chronicle: The Story of the People* (New York:

World Publishing, 1972).

186 Kareem Abdul-Jabbar and Alan Steinberg, *Black Profiles in Courage: A Legacy of African-America Achievement* (New York: Perennial Books, 2000).

187 Ibid.

188 Helen Rand Parish, *Estebanico* (Trotwood, Ohio: LWF Publications, 1974).

189 Jeremie Samuel, *Do You Know Estevanico? Adventures of the World's Greatest Explorer* (New York: Create Space, 2016).

190 Minister of Information JR, "Class is in session: an interview wit' rapper Professor A.L.I.," May 20, 2011, https://bit.ly/3Hmn2O6.

191 Amy Lowe, "The Journey of Estebanico, the Moor," *A Story Rarely Told*, YouTube, 2021, https://bit.ly/3zY3o7b.

192 *Cortés, with the Moorish Soldier Estevanico, Entering Mexico*, ca. 1550, Mexican School, Bibliotheque Nationale, Paris, France.

193 For more on the kachina, see J. Brent Ricks, *Kachinas: Spirit Beings of the Hopi* (Albuquerque: Avanyu Publishing, 1993).

194 Ibid., 11–16.

195 José Cisneros, *Cabeza de Vaca and His Three Companions on the Texas Coast* (Kindle Editions, 2019).

196 Ibid.

197 Ibid.

198 Ted DeGrazia, *Cabeza de Vaca* series is featured in Andrés Reséndez, *A Land So Strange: The Epic Journey of Cabeza de Vaca* (New York: Basic Books, 2007).

199 Ibid.

200 The work stands before the Texas State Capitol in Austin, Texas.

201 McKenna Kelley, "Exploring Estevanico," *South Tampa Bay Magazine*, May 25, 2018, https://bit.ly/3br90wF.

202 Bust of Álvar Núñez Cabeza de Vaca, Museo de Puerto Iguazu.

203 Dr. Robert Goodwin, *Crossing the Continent 1527–1450: The Story of the First African in American History* (New York: Harper Perennials, 2009).

204 Emma Schkloven, "Looking Deeper at the Massive New Juneteenth Mural in Galveston," *Houstonia*, June 18, 2021, https://bit.ly/3c07stR.

205 Favata, 47. In the Muslim faith, there are ninety-nine names for Allah. Most of these are attributes like *Al-Aziz* or "Almighty" and *Al-Alim* or "All-Knowing." Others are titles like *Al-Malik*or "The King" and *Al-Ghaffar* or "He Who Forgives."

206 Anonymous, "The 1539 Marcos de Niza's Expedition," *Planetary Science*, November 15, 2010. Anonymous, "de Niza Expedition," *Associated Press*,

July 12, 2017.

207  The myth of the Seven Cities of Gold began sometime in the late fifteenth century, shortly after Christopher Columbus' first voyage in 1492. In more modern times, Scrooge McDuck and his nephews discover the seven cities of gold in the comic *The Seven Cities of Cibola*. Richard Egan starred in the 1955 film *Seven Cities of Gold*. It also featured Anthony Quinn and Michael Rennie.

208  Favata, 92–94.

209  Ibid., 93.

210  Ibid., 94.

211  Ibid.

212  Ibid., 99–100.

213  Adolph Frances Alphonse Bandelier, *Historical Documents relating to New Mexico, Nueva Vizcaya and Approaches Thereto, to 1773* (Philadelphia: Franklin Classics, 2018).

214  Carl Sauer, *The Road to Cibola* (London: Hassell Street Press, 2021).

215  Henry Wagner, "de Niza Exploration to Cibola," *New Mexico Historical Review*, 1932.

216  Lansing Bloom, "Fray Marcos de Niza and His Journey to Cibola," *New Mexico Historical Review* 3, no. 4 (1947): 415–486.

217  "de Niza Stone," South Mountain, Arizona, discovered in 1922.

218  Author's translation.

219  Favata, 150–151.

220  Ibid., 151.

221  Ibid., 123–124.

222  Ibid., 141.

223  For more on Juan Garrido, see Juan Garrido Otaola, *Ser O No Ser: Lidner Un Diologo Con Tu Futuro Yo* (Madrid: Respendaldos Libros, 2018).

224  Senor Dorantes gave Estevanico his freedom before the pair came to Mexico City.

225  Viceroy Mendoza gave his instructions to Fray de Niza and Estevanico on May 5, 1539.

226  Josaphat Kubayanda, *On Colonial/Imperial Discourse and Contemporary Critical Theory*. By "philosophical foundations of 1619 Project and Critical Race Theory," we mean Marxism.

227  Rolena Adorno, "Estevanico's Legacy: Insights into Colonial Latin American Studies from Postcolonial Africa," *Guided History* (Boston, 1997).

228  Melville J. Herskovits study on the ancestors of Black Americans, discussed

in Edwin R. Embree *Brown America: The Story of a New Race* (New York, 1931).

229   See, Nikole Hannah-Jones, *The 1619 Project* (New York: One World Books, 2021); and Richard Delgado, *Critical Race Theory: An Introduction*, Third Edition (New York: NYU Press, 2017).

230   Anonymous, "Historic World Leaders" (Detroit: Gale Research Project, 1994).

231   Jonathan Gordon, "Ten Great Explorers in History," *History Answers*, March 29, 2019, https://bit.ly/3yxxzQ7.

232   *Relación De Álvar Núñez Cabeza De Vaca*, ed. Enrique Peña (New York: Wentworth Press, 2018).

233   Ponce de Leon arrived in what became St. Augustine, Florida, in April 1513.

234   For more on Juan Garrido, see Jose Luis Garcia Delgado, *Lecciones de Economia espanola* (Madrid: Aranzadi, 2021).

235   Ibid., 937–938.

236   Ibid., 940–944.

237   Meg Smith, "African-American Men," *The Washington Post*, January 7, 2015.

238   Ibid.

239   In the Hebrew Bible, Zipporah appears on several occasions, including Exodus 2:21–22 and 4: 20, Exodus 18:1–4, and Numbers 12 and 21. The narrative about the foreskin is in Exodus 4:25.

240   For more on Mattheus de Souza, see Stephen Vicchio, *Muslim Slaves in the Chesapeake, 1634 to 1865* (Minneapolis: Wisdom Editions, 2019), 11–14. Also see David S. Bogen, "Mathias de Sousa: Maryland's First Colonist of African Descent," *Maryland Historical Society Magazine* 96, no. 1, (2001), 68–85. Several Maryland state documents are also extant about the life of Mattheus de Sousa, including Land Office Record MSA A S920, Sections 1, 19, 20 and 37. General Assembly Upper House Record 1637–1658. MSA S-977-1 Land Office Record, a document that listed De Sousa as a "Molato," MSA S920-4.

241   For more on Dr. Lucas Santomee, see *History of Minorities in Medicine* (Birmingham: University of Alabama Press, 2022), https://bit.ly/3c8scQc. Also see "Enriching Medicine Through Diversity," AMSA, May 26, 2015.

242   De Sousa was definitely a Muslim. We are less certain about Dr. Santomee, but he does have an Arabic surname.

243   Smith, "African-American Men."

244   For more on Onesimus, see Kathryn S. Koo, "Strangers in the House of God:

Cotton Mather, Onesimus, and an Experiment in Christian Slaveholding," *American Antiquarian Society* (2007) 143–175, https://bit.ly/3IHAzhT.

245 George Kittredge, *Some Lost Works of Cotton Mather* (Oxford Palala Press, 2015), 42–44.

246 Andrés Reséndez, *The Other Slavery* (New York: Mariner Books, 2017).

247 Favata, 19–21.

248 Giovanni Ramusio, *Delle Navigazioni e Viaggi* (Rome: KKIEN, 2015).

249 Henri Ternaux-Compans, *Voyages, Relations, and Memories* (Paris, 1837).

250 Frances "Fanny" Bandelier, *Historical Documents Related to New Mexico* (Philadelphia: Franklin Classics, 2018).

251 Enrique Pena, *Relación de Álvar Núñez Cabeza de Vaca* (New York: Wentworth Books, 2018).

252 Favata.

253 *The Account of Cabeza de Vaca: A Literal Translation with Analysis and Commentary*, trans. David Carson (Albuquerque: Living Waters Specialties, 2018).

254 Favata, 100.

255 Arthur Scott Aiton, *Antonio de Mendoza, First Viceroy of New Spain* (Dallas: Southern Methodist University Press), 91–92.

256 Pedro de Castenada Najera, *Narrative of the Coronado Expedition* (New York: Lakeside Publishers, 2002).

257 George Parker Winship, *The Journey of Coronado, 1540–1542* (Oxford: Palala Press, 2016).

258 Hernando de Alarcón, *Documentos Ineditos* in *Conservapedia* (July 13, 2016).

259 Ibid., 17.

260 Cleve Hallenbeck, *Alvar Nunez Cabeza de Vacca: The Journey and the Route of the First European to Cross the Continent of North America, 1534–36* (London: Kennikat Press, 1940).

261 Peter Gerhard, "A Black Conquistador in Mexico," *Hispanic American Historical Review* 58, no. 3 (1978): 451–459.

262 Ruth Pike, "Sevillian Society in the Sixteenth Century: Slaves and Freedmen," *Hispanic American Historical Review*, 47, no. 3 (1967): 358.

# Index

Tucker, William  1–2, 12, 122
Tumius  16
Twilight, Alexander Lucius  124

U

Ulibahall, Georgia  1
Umayyad  15–16, 50, 134, 137

V

Vacapa, Mexico  110, 138
Velázquez, Diego de Cuéllar  121
Venice, Italy  2, 127
Virginia  2, 4, 11–13, 15, 35, 55, 114–116
Voltaire  106, 114
  *Candide*  106, 114

W

Wagner, Henry  111
Walid the First, al-  15
Washington, George  119
Wattasid dynasty  42, 52, 138
wigwams  83
Winship, George Parker  128

Y

Yang, Jeffrey  91
Yaqui Tribe  63, 86
Yumbe  79

Z

Zaouia of Telouet  53
Zayam, Moulay  19, 135
Zia Pueblo  80
Zuni Indians  3, 5, 24–25, 29–34, 65–70,
        72–73, 76–77, 81, 86–87, 97–98,
        100, 102, 109–110, 115, 118,
        129–130, 134, 137–138
Zuni Pueblo  66, 72, 76, 110

# About the Author

Before his retirement in 2016, Stephen Vicchio taught for more than forty years at the University of Maryland, Johns Hopkins, St. Mary's Seminary in Baltimore, and other universities in Britain and the United States. He has authored over three dozen books, as well as essays and plays, mostly about the Bible, philosophy and theology. Among his books since 2000 is his interpretation of the Book of Job; *The Antichrist: A History*; *Biblical Figures in the Islamic Faith*; and books about the religions of American presidents George Washington, Thomas Jefferson and Abraham Lincoln, including *Ronald Reagan's Religious Beliefs*. *Estevanico: The First Black Man in America* is his fortieth book.

www.ingramcontent.com/pod-product-compliance
Lightning Source LLC
Chambersburg PA
CBHW032226080426
42735CB00008B/727